P9-CNF-377

HOW CHURCHES GROW

By the same author

The Bridges of God—A Study in the Strategy of Missions

First published 1955
Reprinted 1957

World Dominion Press, London
Friendship Press, New York

Multiplying Churches in the Philippines

Church Growth and Group Conversion

Case Studies in Church Growth

c/o World Mission
222 S. Downey Avenue
Indianapolis
Indiana, U.S.A.

HOW CHURCHES GROW

The New Frontiers of Mission

DONALD ANDERSON McGAVRAN

WORLD DOMINION PRESS
59 Bryanston Street
Marble Arch
London, W.1

World Dominion Press
59 Bryanston Street
Marble Arch
London, W.1

First published 1959
Reprinted 1963

Distributed in the United States by
Friendship Press
New York

PRINTED IN GREAT BRITAIN BY
THE SHENVAL PRESS LTD.
LONDON, HERTFORD AND HARLOW

CONTENTS

PART I

What This Book is About

PART II

Population Factors in Church Growth

PART III

General Factors in Church Growth

PART IV

Methods of Church-Growth

PART V

Organization in Church-Growth

INTRODUCTION

This is an excellent and much needed book. It will be of great use in the overhauling which missionary strategy must receive. This approach will, of course, evoke many new problems, but the emphasis on a more spontaneous, mobile way of mission is greatly needed.

Although I would often have said the same things in a different way—Dr. McGavran's way is frequently better than mine would have been—I agree wholeheartedly with the purpose of this volume, rejoice in its publication in England and America, and hope it will soon be translated into some European languages.

May 1st, 1959 HENDRIK KRAEMER

Driebergen, Holland

PART I

WHAT THIS BOOK IS ABOUT

I

THE BLAZE OF OPPORTUNITY

The world today is a new and strange place. Men and women long attached to old faiths and loyalties are now confronted with new scientific truth, world civilization, new visions of abundant life, principles of democracy, and the revolutionary revelation of God in Christ. Jolted out of old adjustments and set social, political, economic, and religious patterns, they are searching for better, truer, or more satisfying ways.

We, who are Christians, face a supremely important fact, namely that it is now possible, as it has never been before and may not be again, to give this world of people such a glimpse of the radiant personality of Christ, that instead of saying, "There is no God," or of declaring, "We will give our allegiance to the gods of our ancestors," they will gladly declare, "Jesus is our Lord and Saviour. Through the years ahead we will grow in likeness to Him and devotion to His ways and to His Church."

Adjacent to many of these men and women are missions or younger Churches. The readiness of many of these people to receive Christ means that many existing Churches can grow tremendously and that many new congregations can be established. Quadrupling the number of congregations and Christians in the next ten years is now possible in some areas. Doubling the number is possible in others. Somewhat less growth can be achieved by a large number of missions and younger Churches. In most lands one can without difficulty find areas of receptivity, each with existing church memberships of from, say, 100,000 down to 2,000.[1]

In the neighbourhood of such Churches we no longer have to wonder how growth will occur. Some congregations there are demonstrating it. Missions no longer have to be limited to activities which may, they hope, prepare the people some day to accept Christ. They can, if they wish, now engage in instructing and baptizing converts, organizing churches, and training ministers—i.e. in the central, continuing task of mission.

All this constitutes a change of climate like the end of an ice age. The severely limiting factor—that "mission" meant work without commensurate growth of the Church—has vanished in area after area. In these, the chill wind of suspicion of the Christian faith has abated. The glaciers of an anti-Christian nationalism have retreated. The sun of faith has risen higher in the heavens. Explain it in whatever metaphor you will, churches can multiply.

This remains true despite the fact that in many other areas church growth is still practically impossible. Suspicion and anti-Christian nationalism have increased. The Churches are under fire. To hold what we have demands constant labour.

Such uneven response has obtained from the beginning. During the years 33 to 48 the Church in Judea grew enormously. Yet it did not touch Phoenicia right next to Judea; and, though the Gospel was being preached by the incomparable Paul himself among the Gentiles of Syria and Cilicia, it did not find any response there worth mentioning in the New Testament.

The proclamation of God's love does not receive uniform or simultaneous response. There are areas of little response and consequently small opportunity for church growth. There are also areas of great response and large opportunity for church growth. The latter are of tremendous significance for mission today. It is with these areas and the relationship of the Church to them that this book is concerned. These are the new frontiers of mission.

How shall we discern opportunities for church growth? One way would be to examine the factors which are necessary to bring it

[1] This is *not* a book about people movements. It is about *church growth* of all kinds. It inspects the growth patterns of many younger Churches. It rejoices in the propagation of the Gospel wherever that occurs—by individual or group decisions, by mission or church labours, in responsive and in irresponsive fields.

about. The seeking love of the Christ-filled Christian, layman, pastor or missionary, with a confident witness to relatives or intimates, is one powerful factor. A sense of desperate need on the part of individuals and whole populations is another. The mysterious action of God in history is a third great factor. As He used the Assyrians in ancient times to soften the heart of Israel, so He uses great events today to prepare peoples to accept Him. There are also scores of other factors.

However, we do not need to engage in an extended evaluation of these to estimate opportunity to grow. There is a plain test which we can use. Where persons who have not been Christians are accepting Christ in sufficient numbers, there the Church has opportunity to grow. Where they are not, it does not. This is essentially an observation of spiritual response. When Paul heard that the Holy Spirit was bringing the Gentiles to discipleship in Antioch, he promptly left Tarsus and went to Antioch. He was using this test to determine where opportunity lay.

Great opportunity for church growth is found fairly well around the world. Japan is a Buddhist country. Buddhists are reputedly irresponsive to Christianity. Christians numbered only half of 1 per cent of the total population in 1940. Yet between 1950 and 1955, in one man's meetings, 286,000 persons signed cards saying that they wished to be Christians. Since most of these did not unite with any church, some churchmen are inclined to dismiss this evidence as not meaningful. But is such dismissal justified? What shall we say of the one Church in Japan which starting with 12 congregations in 1948 increased them to 84 by 1955? By 1955 all these congregations had seminary trained ministers, half were completely self-supporting, and the rest were receiving subsidy under agreement to diminish it 20 per cent a year till after five years none was received. The rate of growth was close to 400 per cent, and we presume that equal opportunity for tremendous growth was open to other Churches which they somehow managed to miss.

People often assert that opportunity exists only among primitive people. Mandarin speaking Chinese cannot possibly be classed as primitive people. Those who came to Formosa with Chiang Kai Shek were the cream of a race known for ability and industry. In China they had not been notably responsive to Christianity. But in

Formosa there is a forceful Christian movement among these exiled Mainlanders. Many illustrations of its vigour can be given. It has increased Southern Baptist church membership from less than 100 in 1949 to over 4,000 in 1955, with another 2,900 under definite instruction for baptism. In 1949 there were 12 Protestant churches in Taipei. In 1955 there were over 80 and most of the increase was from Mandarin speaking mainlanders. Gilan is a small town in north-east Formosa. In 1950 there were some 60 mainland Christians meeting occasionally there. Five years later that congregation numbered over 200 and had developed seven branches each with 30 to 80 members.

Is opportunity found in a nominally Roman Catholic population? In Puerto Rico in 1933 the Disciples of Christ numbered about 1,100. In 1955 they numbered about 6,500. This sixfold increase in twenty-two years occurred among a literate and cultured population, despite considerable emigration to the United States. Had the Church not lost several thousand to the States, the membership would have risen to over 8,000. The Assemblies of God have shown a still more striking increase in Puerto Rico.

Primitive tribal peoples also can present an opportunity. Rapid growth among them is sometimes found. A million Yorubas in western Nigeria have become Christian in the last hundred years. Some 40,000 Africans have become Christian in the West Kenya Mission of the American Friends and now compose the largest Annual Meeting of the Society of Friends anywhere in the world. A tremendous discipling has taken place in Uganda in the last sixty years. In Mondombe, Africa, annual baptisms of over 4,000 adults marked the period 1950 to 1954. In the last few years, in one section of British Borneo, a movement has brought 3,000 into the Church and appears likely to bring in all the rest of the tribe—90,000 persons—in the near future. In numbers involved and character achieved, the Lutheran disciplings in New Guinea remind one of the growth of the early Church in Jerusalem.

All the instances mentioned above are illustrations of churches which quadruple their numbers in ten years. What opportunity!

Not all opportunities result in such rapid growth. The occasions on which the Church doubles in a decade are more numerous than where it quadruples. Cases where it increases by half are even more common. The entire Evangelical Christian community in Japan during the last decade has increased by slightly more than half. In Thailand, where church growth has been very small and there are today only 20,000 Protestant Christians in a land of 20 million people, there is one province where the churches have doubled in the last decade. That one province with its open opportunity now contains a fourth of all the Protestants in Thailand. In Formosa the Presbyterian Church is composed of Amoy speaking Formosans. Between 1947 and 1953 its South Synod increased from 10,632 to 14,860. It then planned to double its Amoy speaking membership by 1965. Early in 1956 it was ahead of its schedule. In India the Baptists in a certain field, observing that one of the castes was responsive, concentrated work there and in three years lifted a membership of 3,000 to 4,300. In the Philippines the Baptists around Iloilo increased their membership 25 per cent in three years, 1954–1956, chiefly by conversions from the world. If, over a ten-year period they continue the processes which yield such increase they will have grown by over 100 per cent. In Latin America there are numerous Protestant Churches now growing at 50, 100 and more per cent. Opportunity is everywhere!

Even these illustrations of church growth do not indicate the true magnitude of the opportunity, because the present degree of growth is taking place under the command of a major idea, valid enough in days gone by—that of going everywhere and preaching the Gospel expecting that the increase will be slow and rather disappointing and feeling that rapid increase is somehow discreditable! What would not happen if we were to step out from under the shadow of that major idea and concentrate on discipling responsive populations—both cultured and backward—bringing a maximum number of individuals into the Redemptive Fellowship, and sometimes claiming whole populations for Christ? As the World Church turns toward the multitudes who can be won for Christ, and marches forward under the Great Commission to make disciples of all *nations*, a new magnitude of church growth will blaze forth.

The opportunity is not "*to carry on* church and mission work" but "*to church the responsive unchurched* in as great numbers and as rapidly as possible." Why should any live—or die—without the Saviour? Our eyes will see today's opportunities in their true dimension if we will but think of population after population, where the churches, even under established methods, are growing a little, in terms of discipling the entire population. Readers can do this for many fields with which they are acquainted. For a trial run, let us do it for Africa.

We have long thought of Africa as "a mission field" in which, against great odds of health and climate, church work was being carried on and missionaries were bravely proclaiming the Gospel. Let us now think of Africa as a continent which God wants discipled in this generation. Despite many problems and difficulties, whose seriousness cannot be gainsaid, let us think of so leading Africans into churches that by the year 2000 all Africa south of the Sahara will be as completely discipled as any country in the West. Let us observe the seven reasons which make such an outcome possible.

(1) A rapidly growing younger Church of 20 million has been established largely within the last fifty years. This Church contains almost all the educated Africans. Rulers, too, such as the Premier of the new born state of Ghana and the President of Liberia, are Christians, to say nothing of the very large number of African gentlemen in high government posts, chiefs, and leaders of great influence.

(2) A vast exodus from animism is going on which will hand over scores of millions to other faiths—or no faith—in the next thirty years. Not since the animistic tribes of northern Europe marched out of their old faiths into Christianity has there been anything like it—and this is a much larger exodus taking place in a much shorter time. Between 60 and 80 million people are going somewhere before the year 2000. It may be to materialism, Communism, Islam, Roman Catholicism, or Evangelical Faith, but they are on the march.

(3) The rising economic potential of Africa makes it relatively easy for the pastorate to be self-supporting from the beginning and for church income to rise with the rising income of the membership. This is a practical factor of vast import. The African churches are now self-supporting and will be increasingly so in the years ahead.

(4) The strong sense of community, the tribalism which is the life of Africans, makes group accessions available to speed sound church growth. A trickle of converts, each ostracized by his family as he is baptized, is unnecessary in Africa. Converted men can come in with groups of the converted from their families, their clans, and their villages. This makes for sound growth and buttresses self-support.

(5) Present peaceful conditions are favourable for church growth. Such prominence has been given to both the Mau Mau uprising and apartheid in South Africa that many otherwise well informed churchmen think that Africa, blazing with resentment, is a difficult field for church growth. That there is discontent, mounting to resentment here and there, is obvious; but one has only to compare the conditions of China, Burma, Indonesia, or even Colombia with those in Africa to see that, by and large, African conditions favour church growth. Even in Kenya, by contrast with the Mau Mau uprising, Christianity has appeared so desirable that one outcome of the trouble there has been a great influx into and revival of the churches.

(6) Many governments in Africa are friendly to the idea of discipling the people. In 1954 the governor of the Equatorial Province of Belgian Congo declared that Christianity was the basis of civilization and that his government's policy was to make available the benefits of Christianity to as many of the people as wished to embrace it. Governments are carrying out the educational task in country after country in Africa largely through missions. The school-book business, for example, which involves providing millions of books of all kinds, is largely in the hands of church book-stores.

(7) Finally, it has now been universally recognized that, despite their primitiveness in many remote areas, Africans are potentially as able a race as any, and their discipling is as desirable as any.

These seven favourable conditions mean that vast numbers of growing churches can now be established and that the conversion to Christian faith of Africa south of the Sahara is possible in the foreseeable future. Eighty million persons may be claimed for Christ in the next forty years. No such open door has ever faced Christendom. Here is a continent which may be brought into the kingdom of Christ in this generation. Here "missions" mean reaping the harvest, winning 90 per cent of the population to Christian faith and co-operating with national Churches, which, forty years from now, will comprise a majority of the total population of Africa and of all non-occidental Christians of the world. The momentous nature of this opening towers above the horizon like the Matterhorn.

Africa is only one of many openings, though others may not be as extensive. And why should not such openings occur? God reigns. Where Christ has been proclaimed for scores of years and His churches demonstrate His wonderful way of life, is it not to be expected that some populations at least will respond; that a wave will run through them making them friendly to the idea of embracing Christianity? Opportunities are all about us. If we can but lift our minds above the routine of organization and the harassing round of stationary duties, we shall see them.

Those who labour among men who have set their faces like flint against the Gospel may say, "We do not believe that there is any great responsiveness. At least not here. Why does not God bring responsiveness everywhere?" The answer might be that until the Churches begin claiming for Christ those populations which can now be won, why should God cause others to respond.

A revolutionary world will bring about a new responsiveness among people now on the edge of or intermeshed with existing Churches. The kaleidoscopic changes in the world of today cannot be foretold. A few years ago who would have guessed the present position of Pakistan or Pekin? Changes in reverse might as easily occur. The Church may go back into China sooner than we think, and when it does the significance of the Mainlander Churches of Formosa today will be terrific. A turn of the wheel and what happens in Thailand, a shift in the line and what happens in Russia! Our anxiety need not be for lack of opportunity for church growth. Our anxiety must concern our lack of faith and imagination, our slow inadequate response to great openings.

It may be objected that in this chapter we have built up an impression that great church growth is possible by amassing examples of particular areas where spectacular growth is occurring, and that this is really illegitimate because great increases will be ironed out by the slow growth of other areas. Precisely this has been true of the past. In an era which has not focused on church growth, but has carried on good church and mission work everywhere, regardless of response, great growth is constantly averaged against no growth. This, however, will continue true only on one assumption—that we continue to send as many reapers to cold unproductive fields as we send to those waving with yellow grain. If, on the contrary, we begin to work to a new pattern, focus on church growth, learn all we can about it, and concentrate on winning the winnable now, the whole rate of church growth can be radically increased. If the whole available resources of missions and younger Churches were poured into existing responsive populations, they would still fall short of that maximum productivity of which they are capable.

Opportunity blazes today, but it may be a brief blaze. Certainly conditions which create the opportunity—as far as human wisdom can discern—are transient conditions. We have today. Let us move forward.

II

THE CRUCIAL ISSUE IN THE WORLD MISSION

In the midst of the unparalleled opportunity just recounted, most younger Churches and their assisting missions are not achieving much church growth. Christians comprise 2 per cent of the population in India, 1 per cent in China, ½ per cent in Japan, two-fifths of 1 per cent in Thailand and even less in many other lands. Christians are not only a minute minority in the population, but their proportion increases very slowly if at all. Christians have grown from about 1 million to about 10 million in India during the last century, while the population has grown from about 100 million to about 400 million! This lack of growth is in spite of much excellent work by younger Churches and missions.

They are improving their organizational efficiency, deepening the spiritual life of the membership, and serving their fellow men with admirable consecration. But they do not usually achieve great growth.

Hundreds of such illustrations could be given. A Church of 10,000 in 1850 now numbers 12,000. A Church of 2,500 in 1925, thirty years later numbers 2,592. A Church of 120,000 in 1930 had 130,000 in 1955. Cessation of church growth is a commonplace among the younger Churches. There are, to be sure, encouraging exceptions, some of which I have already mentioned, but, broadly speaking, growth is not commensurate with the effort applied and the opportunity afforded.

Furthermore, this lack of growth excites no adverse comment. Missions and younger Churches too often contentedly care for what they have. A great missionary society has poured large resources into four provincial Churches in India despite the fact that their growth has averaged only 16 per cent a decade. Its fifth provincial Church, which has grown a healthy 150 per cent a decade for thirty years, has received less than 5 per cent of the society's resources. During the last seventeen years this society has spent $1,700,000 in the assistance of four Churches whose total membership of 15,322 in 1926 increased to only 22,000 by 1954. It has poured out this treasure and accompanying life without searching for ways to increase church growth or transferring resources to where its churches *are* growing and could grow much more. There has been no perceptible sorrow over such small increase. Facing the annual expenditure of about 100,000 dollars and practically no church growth, the society, its missionaries, and the younger Churches it assists have all shown considerable complacency. This is a commonplace pattern of action. For many today, "missions" apparently means doing good church and mission work whether the churches multiply or not.

This can be documented on every hand. For example, the 1956 catalogue of a famous graduate school for the training of missionaries lists eighty courses of which only five have anything to do with the Church abroad, and they, at least so the catalogue seems to say, do not deal with the increase of members and churches—imperative though that is. This contentedness with by-passing the central business of mission is commonplace. Missionary training schools teach about other religions, other cultures, the health of missionaries, phonetics, languages, Communism, anthropology, sociology, psychology—but they do not have much to say about how churches multiply, how men are converted, or what factors make for sound and rapid growth of the churches.

Immediately after the I.M.C. Conference at Willingen in 1952, Dr R. Pierce Beaver penned the following sentences which the Division of Foreign Missions published:

> The delegates at Willingen say, as they reviewed the situation of the Church around the world today, that the missionary enterprise is in great measure a colossal system of inter-church aid, with relatively little pioneer evangelistic advance.

This terrific assessment frightened no one. "The colossal system of inter-church aid" passes for good missions—whether the younger Churches grow or not. If we are aiding them, that is good mission policy. The "no-growth" situation is accepted without remorse. Indeed, it would be immediately claimed that missions are doing much more important things than winning men to Christ and multiplying churches.

Five great drives have characterized missions during the last thirty years. Each has been designed to make the world programme of the Church more effective. Each claimed to be the way to greater church growth.

The first drive was to broaden the base of missions to include every area of human life. "A mighty Church awake to needy humanity and serving mankind" was the slogan. Missions thus broadened became intricate and complex operations with many parts. The supposition was that each part was necessary to the growth of the Church. But adequate church growth has not generally occurred, is not occurring, and does not seem likely to occur under this present system.

The second drive correctly changed almost complete missionary leadership to almost complete national leadership. In younger Churches, one after another, nationals came into control. But there is today no positive correlation between such control and church growth. Devolution has not been accompanied by church growth. Where this was going on before it has sometimes continued. Where there was little before there is usually little today.

The third drive was for special types of missions. A tremendous amount of life has been poured out in rural reconstruction, literacy, public health, and relief work. Yet the evidence clearly shows that these have little to do with the multiplication of churches. Where such multiplication would have taken place anyhow, there, to be sure, growth has occurred. But this drive to improve social conditions has not generally caused increase or even been conducted in places where ingathering was possible.

The fourth drive in which the missionary world has rejoiced, was for the formation of the International Missionary Council and more recently the World Council of Churches. Great resources have been devoted to these agencies, and their meetings have been widely heralded and publicized. They have done much good. All Christians can thank God for them. But it cannot be claimed that they have led their affiliates into great church growth. Indeed, it is commonly heard that the Churches of the West unaffiliated with the International Missionary Council and the World Council of

Churches have shown greater growth with less resources. Certainly that is true in some places.

Fifth, the drive for church union has perhaps elicited more enthusiasm than any other one aspect of the Christian enterprise. One of the main arguments for union advanced by younger Church leaders and others has been that the divided state of Christendom inhibited growth and church union would stimulate it. Unfortunately figures of church increase do not support the argument. United Churches are not achieving greater or more rapid increase than others.

Despite these drives, which to many churchmen are the sum total of missions, the younger Churches and their assisting missions are not producing church growth commensurate with the effort expended and the opportunities which God places before us. While across the world here and there cases of great ingathering have occurred, which have lifted the average church growth for an entire country a little and have provided protagonists of modern missions with many illustrations of achievement, nevertheless on the whole growth has been disappointing. Where growth of 50 per cent a decade was possible, only 10 per cent has been achieved; where 100 per cent was possible, a mere 40 per cent has been achieved; and where 1,000 per cent could have been reached, we have rejoiced in a pitiful 200 per cent a decade. How could it be otherwise? The main resources have not been devoted to church growth, and none of the changing emphases in missions has seriously sought church growth where it could be found.[1]

Facing such inadequate growth, why not take the easy way out and brush the whole subject off, declaring that we are not interested in "mere numerical increase of the Church"? Unfortunately it will not be thus easily dismissed. The fact of the matter is that membership increase is absolutely central to the life of younger Churches and missions.

They themselves proclaim it so. Church after Church, mission

---

[1] Here and throughout this book, facing the common self-deception which easily proclaims "numerical increase of the Church does not interest us," we have consciously omitted many good things about these drives and the world mission which should be said, and have consciously overemphasized the case for the centrality of church growth. This emphasis is needed today. We earnestly trust it will not be tomorrow.

after mission, conferences, assemblies, and grand councils meet in ceaseless procession to affirm their dedication to winning the world for Christ. Evangelistic departments are maintained. Evangelistic budgets are raised and spent. All other emphases in missions, from agriculture through medicine and education, expressly declare that their main task is to make Christ known through their special media. More missionaries are sent abroad by younger and older Churches than ever have been before. More money is poured into missionary effort than would have been thought possible twenty years ago. The intention to make available the abundant life of Jesus Christ our Lord, to multiply His Church, and to extend the benefits of Christianity to all mankind appears unshaken and central.

In face of huge numbers of God's children without knowledge of Him church growth is essential. Where the population of a land such as Sweden or Scotland has been discipled (the towns and villages are full of church buildings, theological seminaries flourish in every province, and all groupings of citizens have at least large minorities of earnest Christians in them) *there* some might hold that increase in numbers was of secondary importance; but where only two in 100, or one in 100, or often only one in 1,000 are Christians, there surely numerical increase of Christians is the first task of the Church.

When our Lord commands us to make disciples of the nations, He surely does not consider the job successfully concluded when one in 100 has yielded Him allegiance. Burying even 1 or 2 per cent in a napkin to return to Him after thirty years, still 1 or 2 per cent, will scarcely merit His "well done."

Nor can it be safely supposed that better living, a more Christian social order, The Kingdom of God on earth, a vast increase of brotherhood, justice, and peace can be obtained while only one in 100 is a church member. That would be impossible in Tennessee. Why blithely imagine it possible in Thailand?

We of the West are greatly concerned about boys and girls growing up without Christian instruction in our own cities where they daily pass by the doors of a dozen churches. We should, in truth, be concerned about these. But what about others? We cannot forget that unless the younger Churches and their assisting missions achieve enormous church growth, now increasingly possible, hundreds of millions of boys and girls will continue to grow up without ever hearing of Christ. They will pass the door of no church in their entire lifetime.

Growth in numbers is essential for self-support. A Church in Latin America has eight self-supporting churches of 200 to 600 members each, twenty heavily subsidized churches of about sixty members each, and twenty-two little branch congregations averaging twenty-two communicants. Many younger Churches all around the world are similarly made up of a few strong and many small and scattered churches. These latter, if they would be self-supporting and survive when mission assistance declines, must grow. Future churches too, except in successful people movements, are certain to start as small groups of Christians which will become self-supporting only as they increase in numbers. In every Church which has numerous small congregations the current desirable drive for a highly educated ministry, supported by the Church, cannot be successful except on the basis of a greatly expanded membership. To support an educated ministry the little congregations must grow.

Growth in numbers is also essential for normal community life. It is easy for Christian leaders, living in large Christian communities and experiencing all the securities, satisfactions and benefits of abundant social intercourse, to decry "growth in mere numbers" and to praise "growth in maturity and spirituality"; but they might not speak so readily if they had regularly to worship with only a handful of illiterates, if they could find no Christian wives for their sons, or if a burial service for their dead depended on the arrival of Christians from many miles away.

Man-in-society is the normal man. Solitary Christians or small bands of separated Christians can and do exist after a fashion, specially when buttressed by loving missionary fellowship; but if they do not gather to themselves a community sufficiently large to provide social requirements, they live a partial life and their survival through several generations is questionable.

Take it any way at all, increase of members and congregations is absolutely essential to the world mission of the church.

There is a difficulty here which we must frankly face. This axiomatic proposition involves a corollary that numerical increase is a chief criterion of the welfare of the younger Churches. This corollary is entirely sound; yet it is distasteful to some Christians. To them it looks mechanical and seems to slight spiritual development. Let us discern what numerical increase is not and is.

It is not adding mere names to the roll or baptizing those who have no intention of following Christ. Roll-padding, aside from being dishonest, is useless. The numerical increase worth counting is that which endures from decade to decade. Roll-padding and dishonest baptizing will never produce lasting growth.

Numerical increase presupposes and necessitates good spiritual care. No Evangelical Church can grow greatly in numbers which has a programme unsuited to men's needs. Men turn to those places where their actual needs are met. True, it is possible for them to be swept into some congregation, but unless they receive real food they will not stay there. Growing Churches are precisely those whose members believe they enjoy a life superior to that they had before. Otherwise men would neither come in nor stay. A Church whose membership grows by leaps and bounds needs no more convincing proof that its programme suits the actual needs of its congregation.

Numerical increase is not the only criterion of success. Other matters must be taken into account. Church development is like that of a child. Adequate nutrition, a maturing social awareness, and intelligence are desirable elements in development; but were a child's weight to remain at fifty-six pounds for several years, the mother would rightly feel anxious, no matter how socially mature the child was! The one criterion—increase of body weight—is not enough; but to disregard weight as a chief criterion is fatal. Yet this is often done in ecclesiastical matters—growth in membership is not regarded as a chief consideration in estimating church welfare. Church leaders take disastrous comfort in clichés that "while the Church is not growing, of course, it is maturing—or developing in self-consciousness, or deepening its spiritual life, or becoming more indigenous." Where great growth is possible and not occurring the thought that "all is well, for we are concentrating on the spiritual" is an opiate inducing a false sense of well being. The factor of lack of growth is being completely ignored.

In lands where the Churches can grow, growth in numbers is a good test as to whether Christians really share the mind of Christ.

He had compassion on the multitudes and gave His life for them while they were still outside the Church. Can we do less? The Book of Acts records numbers with great care. They were an important aspect of Church growth. They still are today. Not the only aspect, to be sure; but an aspect which must never be left out of mind when evaluating any given Church.

Churchmen then who are interested in numbers of Christians, the rate of church multiplication, and the processes by which a nation is discipled or a countryside catches fire for God, are right.

Thus we come to our central consideration. In a world of hundreds of millions without Christ, how can the Churches and their assisting missions achieve adequate church growth? What makes churches grow? What makes them stop growing? What are assisting missions doing which promotes growth? Are they doing anything which prevents it? How can the younger Churches use the massive resources of the older Churches for significant church multiplication? These questions are crucial for the world task of both the older and the younger Churches. They merit our closest attention.

III

OBSTRUCTIONS IN THE PROTESTANT MIND

Tragically the centrality and opportunity of great church growth, stressed in the last two chapters, are frequently neither seen nor acknowledged. Some readers may already have muttered to themselves, "Tremendous pother about mere numbers. There are many things more important than size." The ability to look great opportunity for church growth squarely in the face and not see it is common. Three basic structures of thought in the Protestant mind block reception and prevent recognition of the significance of the wide open doors. To identify these thought-structures will be helpful.

I. The methods and slogans of the transient, exploratory phase of missions (which has been operating so long that it now seems the only correct way of mission) blocks church thinking.[1]

As the Churches around the world awoke to their missionary obligations, they did not wait for natural contacts, but thrust out teams of missionaries into the most distant, different, and unlikely places. Paul's contemporaries of the first century knew from childhood the language and culture of those to whom they carried the Good News. Missionaries of the nineteenth century went deliberately to those whose language they did not know, whose customs seemed utterly strange, and with whom they had normally no

---

[1] It must be remembered that boards, missions, and all concerned have been persistent both in trying to discover better ways of doing the work and in sacrificial and heroic efforts to do it. There have been numerous surveys, repeated visits of secretaries, delegations of laymen and others to the field plus the unremitting toil on the part of Churches, missions, and churchmen—all eager to get a better job done. The introduction of rural reconstruction, hospitals, mass education, and many other new departures have all been planned originally for the purpose of winning people to Christ and establishing a strong indigenous Church. I am proud of the humble part God has given me in this continuing effort. I stress the magnificent foundations which have been laid during the past 150 years.

But as a missionary of the Cross I am deeply concerned that the vast opportunities of today be bought up, and by and large they are not being bought up. In this chapter I ask what keeps us, who are so deeply dedicated to the task and know the work of missions so well, from rushing to buy them up. My answers are certainly not exhaustive. They may not even be correct. But they are an honest attempt to answer the question. Should any disagree with them, I invite him to study the matter on the broadest possible basis, and tell us why the opportunities of today are not resulting in substantial, continuous, and good church growth.

intercourse. Their approach had to be tentative and exploratory. Probing was the order of the day. There was major opportunity for serious misunderstanding.

Consequently (except when a people movement brought large numbers into the Church) the common outcome of the exploratory period of missions was a slow small growth of the Church. Converts were won as individuals and with great difficulty. Orphans were reared. Slaves were bought and freed. Women were rescued. Many of the first Christians were employed as helpers, labourers, teachers, preachers, and translators. Hospitals and schools were started as means of penetrating an indifferent or hostile population and of conserving and enriching the life of the small Christian churches. To the sending churches, missions came to mean "service largely to non-Christians but also to small slowly growing communities of Christians." During what we may call the "ice age" churchmen felt it to be axiomatic that the Church in the mission field grows very slowly. "Missions" to them was gradually presenting the Gospel, sowing in hope, and slowly penetrating an alien culture.

Such slow growth inevitably developed a theology and method of missions to fit it. The essential missionary duty—where the vast majority rejected the Gospel—was witness, whether the hearers believed or not. Appropriate scripture was quoted in support. Boards came to believe that the main thing was to carry on mission work decade after decade even when, despite all efforts, the churches did not grow much. National and missionary leaders of the younger Churches fitted themselves into the various niches and performed various services to the Christian community and to the rejectors of the Gospel; and in doing their departmentalized duties considered their full obligations honourably discharged, even if the unreached multitudes in their neighbourhoods remained unreached and the churches did not increase. Slogans grew up to justify such glacial missions: "One soul is worth all this labour." "God's way is a slow way." "He will give the increase." "We seek re-born men and women, not numbers of converts." "Those who are too free with the water of baptism often repent in the water of tears."

When growth did occur and then stopped, the accepted explanation was that "a period of consolidation must follow a period of growth." People did not recognize that this explanation was really a rationalization for an unnecessary condition. To be fair, many cases of arrested growth were unavoidable at the level of support afforded by the home churches, and with the degree of understanding of church growth which then obtained. *Under such conditions* "stop-and-go" church growth was inevitable. Nevertheless, the explanation given was only a rationalization. The real cause of arrested growth lay in the insufficiencies of the discipling teams.

Back in the exploratory period, acceptance of slow church-growth was doubtless the will of God. Nothing else could have kept Christian missions working in difficult or hostile fields till the small churches became firmly rooted, an indigenous leadership grew up, and both Christians and non-Christians began to understand what Christianity meant. Perhaps more significant than anything else, this exploratory phase of missions lasted till the colonialism of the West ended and Christ could appear to such nations, not as a conqueror, but as the power of God available to all who believed.

Traditional mission policy looks so right to churchmen that they tend to continue it even after conditions have greatly changed. Thus "ice-age" thinking dominates the world of missions today, even where the ice-sheet has melted.

This glorification of slowness, this deep-seated conviction that God works slowly, this investment of literally hundreds of thousands of lives by foreign and national churchmen that a relatively few persons might come to a more genuine Christian faith, has built up a mental structure which cannot acknowledge the importance of great church growth. The tremendous challenge of the open door often cannot be even seen.

II. The second thought-structure which hides the significance of church growth from many Protestants is "Gathered Church Convictions." What are Gathered Churches, and what convictions do they hold?

The World Church today is only two or three centuries out of the iron grip of monopolistic State Churches. Indeed, State Churches still control the religious life of Greece, Spain, Italy, and most Latin American countries. They would rule most of Eastern Europe were it not for an even more monopolistic secular government.

In uninhibited State Churches, the nation is held to coincide with the Church. All citizens are regarded as normally members of the monopolistic Church. Entrance into citizenship and church membership is fundamentally by birth, modified in the Church by infant baptism. Unless excommunicated, a baptized person remains "a Christian" no matter what lack of faith and holy living he manifests. In State Churches to be a Christian had little to do with a personal dedication to Jesus Christ, an infilling of the Holy Spirit, or being born again.

The Gathered Churches rose in a vehement revolt against such nominal Christianity. To them the only true Church is composed of men gathered out of "the world," re-born individuals, knowing themselves to be risen again with Christ. Christ gathers true believers—those who intend to live as His disciples, use the means of grace, and walk in His footsteps—into His Churches. Hence these are called the Gathered Churches.

The Gathered Churches did not rise easily. Violent war went on century after century between State Churches and those who felt that it was sacrilege to give the name "Church" to any assembly of "Christians by birth." The State Churches fought furiously to maintain their monopoly. This is what the inquisitions, burnings and wars were about. This is why Roger Williams left the Old World, and left Massachusetts too. Leaders of the Gathered Churches by hundreds of thousands poured money, labour, and life unstintedly into the battle. In places they were successful and the Gathered Churches hold the door open for the practice of free spiritual Christianity. Not for themselves only. Wherever they have wrested the right to exist from the State Churches, there the latter, to their very great benefit, are compelled at least to some practice of free spiritual Christianity. They are definitely at their best when they must operate in an atmosphere of genuine religious freedom forced on them by the Gathered Churches.

The iron conviction needed by the Gathered Churches, both for risking life and liberty where there was hot war and for enduring studied contempt where there was cold, was not generated by casual considerations of method. It was quarried from the Bible and smelted in the furnaces of theology. Men risk their lives for what they believe is God's will.

During the last 150 years as, through the missionary movement, Christian Churches started anew to carry out the Great Commission, they consciously chose and intentionally practised Gathered Church policies. These had great prestige. They had enabled tremendous strides to be taken toward a fuller embodiment of the life of Christ. They were so obviously right and so obviously based on the Bible. Most missionaries were personally converted men. Even the missions of State Churches believed in and worked for the establishment of Gathered Churches from among non-Christians; Gathered Church convictions and methods were the universal, unquestioned ground of missionary effort.

Missionaries therefore appealed for individuals out of the general population to choose Christ. They called out of the world those who would, of their own free choice, follow Christ. They examined those who wanted to become Christians to make sure that each convert had sufficient knowledge of Christ to enable him to rest his faith intelligently on Him. They refused many. Missionaries were not interested in discipling great populations, thus increasing "the mere number of Christians." Discipline also was exercised freely to purge the Church from those "by whom it is continually encumbered and betrayed." Younger Church leaders too, reared in this tradition, believed that the need was not for more Christians but for better Christians, not for the extension of Christianity, but for the intensification of it.

Such convictions fitted the thought-structure arising out of the exploratory phase of missions. Ice-age missions proclaimed, "The Church must grow very slowly, for opposition and resistance are high. Paganism is so different. Increase will take time. In this generation we shall prove that we are friends. In that generation or the next, people will start becoming Christians. We proclaim Christ by word and kindly deed. God in His own time will give the increase." Gathered Church convictions heartily seconded this pronouncement and added, "Christian character cannot be mass produced. We must build on sure foundations. Nothing unworthy must be allowed in the Church. We cannot be concerned over mere numbers."[1] They took folk in one by one on proof that they had

[1] Those who know their missions can readily quote contrary dicta. There is that famous statement of Jacob Riis who, over 100 years ago, was resisting the closing of a mission because of the appalling mortality among the missionaries. He wrote home, "Though a thousand perish, all Africa must be won for Christ." Yet those who know will, we believe, recognize that our phrasings fairly delineate convictions congenial to the gathered church mind. Jacob Riis himself would have endorsed them.

really been born again. They counted non-growing churches as of equal or superior value to those which grew greatly. Growth in numbers—which is what the State Churches had—was discounted as compared with growth in grace.[1]

In the light of present opportunity of church growth, what can we say in answer to such Gathered Church convictions?

First, that excellent as they are, they do not rightly apply to all populations. They apply chiefly to discipled populations, where they have scored great triumphs. In nominally Christian nations, where there is at least some religious liberty, Gathered Church methods have made outstanding advances.

They have not been notably successful among non-Christian peoples. Indeed, if we exclude Christward people movements from our calculations—and they should be excluded because they have happened despite Gathered Church convictions, not because of them—and concentrate on those Churches in mission lands established according to Gathered Church convictions, we could safely say that Gathered Church methods have been notably unsuccessful.

There is a good reason for this. Except in individualized, urbanized, homogenous populations, men and women exist in social organisms such as tribes, castes, and kindreds. They have an intense people-consciousness and tribal loyalty. Churchmen holding Gathered Church convictions proclaim a universal Gospel to them and invite them as individuals, regardless of what others do, to choose Christ. To them this sounds like being urged to leave their own and join the Christian "tribe." It is as if Brahmans from India were asked to join Negro Churches in South Africa, knowing that their children would inevitably inter-marry with Negroes. "Becoming a Christian" to race-conscious tribes and castes seems more a racial than a religious matter. When, in order to espouse the Christian Faith an individual has traitorously to leave his own race the Church grows slowly. The social organism resists Christianity and heavily penalizes any of its members who breaks away and accepts the invading faith.

Second, undiscipled peoples best become Christians through

[1] Sir Kenneth Grubb in the 1952 *World Christian Handbook* notes that "many of the older Churches of the West remain curiously resistant to any attempt to assess their numerical strength." We presume that ice-age thinking and gathered church convictions lie at the bottom of this resistance.

group conversions and people movements. When conditions are right groups of some people start to accept Christianity. Men become Christians with their families and kinship groups. Many groups, each carefully instructed, across the months and years come into the Church. In a few years or decades the population becomes largely or entirely Christian. It has been discipled.

An undiscipled people prefers to move into any religion in groups. If a people on the march faces both an Evangelical Church, which takes in only a few reborn individuals, and another Church or Faith which encourages groups to come to Christ, the people is likely to go to the second. Indeed, this is happening all the time. Gathered Church convictions look on with equanimity and say, "We don't want that kind of Christians anyway."

Now we all agree that we want genuine Christians. The question is, how can we best get them? Are they more likely to be made out of a discipled people (admittedly babes in Christ, but babes whose house of worship is the Church, whose scripture is the open Bible, whose Lord is Jesus Christ, and whose fellowship is with the World Church) or out of a people whose book, temple, and lord are those of Buddhism, Hinduism, Islam or some non-Evangelical variety of Christianity?

Discipling is a necessary intermediate stage. To allow our Gathered Church convictions to minimize the significance of this intermediate stage is like allowing graduate school standards to hide the significance of enrolling millions of children in elementary schools. There will be little graduate study if millions do not get through elementary school. There will be few Gathered Churches if scores of millions are not discipled first.

Third, the Gathered Church method was not used in the New Testament Church. There we see the passion of Pentecost which rejoiced in 3,000 baptized in a single day and hastened to baptize more and more till a short time later there were 5,000 men (perhaps 20,000 persons) in the Church. The Lord was adding daily to their number, multitudes were believing, and a great company of priests became disciples of Christ. After this, Paul and others continued to gather further multitudes from the synagogue communities around the Mediterranean Sea.

Side by side with this intermediate step, the Holy Spirit, through

Paul and the apostles, put such stress on personal responsibility, individual appropriation of the riches of God in Christ Jesus, search for things which are above, crucifying the flesh, renouncing Satan and all his works, and putting on the whole armour of God, that the discipled companies became full of individuals who were mature in Christ.

As far as the record goes, the Church did not refuse large numbers at any time because they did not fully understand the universality of Christ; did not have a correct view of His atoning death; could not repeat the catechism; kept slaves, or drank liquor. They took all who accepted Jesus as Lord, called them "babes in Christ," and trusted to the Holy Spirit, the fellowship, the teaching, the worship, and the scriptures to perfect those discipled.

Luke did not scorn numbers. He rejoiced in the large numbers becoming Christian and carefully recorded them. The early churches did not scorn numbers. When they heard that multitudes in Samaria had received the Word of God, they gladly sent them Peter and John; and when they heard that in Antioch a great number had believed and turned to the Lord they at once dispatched Barnabas who, when he came and saw, rejoiced.

In regard to large accessions to the Christian Faith, all of us with Gathered Church convictions (and this includes many from the State Churches too) must go back to the New Testament and see how these were handled there. Nothing replaces study of the New Testament at this point. The leaders of the early Church were keenly aware of responsive multitudes and eager to lead them at once into the churches. We find a theology which seeks for multitudes and transforms them.

III. The third thought-structure which hides the opportunity of today is that of "the tall towers of total Christianity." In the last few decades, large numbers of Christian leaders all over the world have studied what it would mean to a civilization to be completely Christian. They think of Christian strategy in terms of perfecting the many facets of life. They argue that if Christians would only create the kind of civilization which Christ could approve, the world would vault immediately out of its present miserable state and into the life of God.

There would be a Christ-ruled social order—an organization of labourers, thinkers, priests, poets, merchants, and rulers in which none could be exploited, none batten on the flesh of others, and all have opportunity for maximum personal development. Land would be so distributed that the tiller was neither slave, serf, nor share-cropper. Every country would be self-governing. There would be no imperial overlords. The Church would represent all classes of society. It would be oriented to factories as well as to offices, and to farms as well as to suburban homes. The benefits of tremendous power—coal, oil, water, and atom—would be distributed equally. Health and education would be within the reach of all. A Christ-dictated relationship between the many races of mankind would obtain. Under the over-arching Fatherhood of God would flourish a genuine brotherhood of man. Christian solutions to war, poverty, and sickness would have banished these scourges. A unified Christ-filled Church would, with a pure heart, adore God and shepherd His people.

"This," they exclaim, "is what Christianity means. How can we possibly think in terms of numerical increase of the present inadequate Christians as a desirable end? What we must be doing is smashing this sorry scheme of things and building it again according to the Master's will. What we need is not more Christians but better Christians. The day demands, not conventional Christians, but radical Christians willing to follow Christ into unexplored fields, to pioneer the Christian way of life against the current of mediocre conformity. To a world in revolution, Christianity must appear the religion *par excellence* for revolutionaries. This kind of Christianity, true both to Christ and to the great needs of men, will almost automatically be accepted." These are, indeed, tall and gleaming towers. They easily hide the rather humble structure of church-growth among the actual peoples of earth. For by far the greatest majority of men are humble folk cultivating two or three acres of land, living on mud-floors, not knowing how to read and write, counting themselves fortunate if they can grow or purchase grain enough to keep hunger from the door, and suffering from many preventable diseases. Humble churches led by humble pastors arise from among these multitudes. All their millions are important to the extension of the reign of God throughout the entire earth.

God loves every man amongst them. They are His children. The more redeemed, the better pleased is God.

Is it, we ask, necessary that the vision of total Christianity blot out the crucially important opportunity for the redemption of increasingly large numbers of humble men? On this point, what shall we say to our tall towers?

At the outset we rejoice in them ourselves and thank God that the day has dawned when men can dream and plan for His rule to control every walk of life. All men, around the world, truly should see these towers. God's plan for a just, peaceful, and brotherly world is the best solution to the world's ills. Christians can be glad that they have such a blueprint.

Yet the only way toward this reconstructed society is reconstructed men. The only certain foundation to a Christ-ruled social order is Christ's rulership in the hearts of the men and women who compose it. A corollary of this truth is that full implementation of total Christianity is impossible till there has been tremendous increase in numbers of real Christians. This increase will have to occur in "Christian" lands where the task is to win men from nominal allegiance to full faith in Christ. It will also have to occur in "non-Christian" lands where the task is more difficult —to win men who do not know Christ at all. The tall towers are built on humble foundations, and can go no higher than the foundations can support.

Some western leaders like to think that if Christians would only practise total Christianity, most of the problems of the world would vanish and men would almost automatically become Christians. This thinking is fallacious. It assumes that there are already Christians enough to dominate the scene. It imagines that Christianity is as powerful everywhere as it is in those countries where a majority are professed Christians.

The difference in degree between a land where church-members are 50 per cent of the population and one where they are half-of-one-per-cent is so great as to become a difference in kind. For example, 6 volts of electricity flowing through an ordinary bulb leave it completely dark, whereas 110 volts transform it into an incandescent light. The difference between 6 volts and 110 is, to be sure, one of degree; but for lighting purposes it is truly one of kind. Similarly, it is vain to expect a minute number of Christians, most of whom are uneducated peasants or employed persons living in rented houses, to bring the blessings of total Christianity to Java, the Sudan, or other similar lands where the Church numbers less than 1 per cent of the population. There must first be a tremendous expansion in the number of Christians.

It has been said that many Christian leaders of the West suffer from delusions of grandeur. Because of the stature of Christianity in their lands, they cannot realize how limited Christianity is where it is a tiny struggling minority and how weak it will continue to be till it becomes a tenth, a fifth, or more of the population.

In the New Testament there is an interesting confirmation of the need for growth prior to great social change. Slavery was widely practised during the first decades of the Christian era. Some Christians were slaves. Other Christians owned slaves. Slavery then was just as abhorrent to God and just as degrading to men as it is today. The New Testament was being written during these very decades. Yet in all its twenty-seven books there is not a single line, not a single word, calling on Christians to do away with the institution of slavery.

Among the possible reasons for this puzzling omission is the practical one that while the Church was a tiny minority of the population, and quite without power to enact social legislation, agitation for a slaveless society would have been useless and, during the very centuries when the Church could grow mightily, would have deflected its attention from its main business, which was to bring multitudes of every land to the abundant life in Christ. Thus the thought of doing away with slavery never occurred to the writers of the New Testament and the Holy Spirit who inspired them reserved that task for a Church which had grown enormously.

There are times when the main business of the Church is to grow. Today, in land after land such a time has arrived—the most urgent and pressing business of the Church there is increase. These are the very days in which that is most possible. By growing, the Church can best bring the blessings of total Christianity to its beloved people. There are also times and places when the main business of the Church is to create social change. Each in its time. There is no need for those correctly advocating social change in one land to decry harvesting responsive populations in another. The sooner great populations follow in His steps, the more effective will social changes be.

At just this point some readers are likely to protest, mentioning some venture which was started by a few Christians and yet triumphed, changing the patterns of life in an entire nation. Most illustrations of this kind will, however, be taken from discipled lands. They pre-suppose at least a nominally Christian population. Other readers may cite social reforms which non-Christian lands have successfully achieved after these had been sparked by minute numbers of Christians. If the Christian way is the better way, then it may be practised by non-Christian societies—after a fashion. Thus Russian Marxists widely advocate, and to a limited degree practise, the brotherhood of man. Full brotherhood escapes them. Because of their materialism it cannot even be seen by them. In further comment on these protests, we might ask whether social advance unaccompanied by faith in Christ is a satisfactory goal for Christians.

Still other readers may protest, recalling the yeast of whose power our Lord Himself spoke. But the leaven lifts the dough only when the yeast cells multiply enormously. Do those walking by the blaze of total Christianity feel that a few cells of yeast can do the job—while remaining a few? Actually a few cells of yeast exercise little lift. Only when they multiply fantastically do they transform the dough.

Fantastic increase in the number of Christians is essential to the achievement of total Christianity. If the world is to become Christ's and fully know the abundant and eternal life, churches must multiply enormously. Consequently, the opportunity to grow is always of high importance to the world programme of the Church. Whenever and wherever it occurs it must be seen and acted on. Neither a method designed perpetually to present the Good News to the irresponsive, nor gathered church convictions, nor the tall towers of total Christianity must be allowed to blot out this central truth.

IV

THE STRUCTURE OF CHURCH GROWTH

The central business of the younger Churches and their assisting missions is church growth. Yet curiously they often know little about its structure or take the trouble to measure it accurately.

Much careful study is required to find out what makes a church grow. Perhaps the easiest way to set about it is to study, say, "Church X in our great mission field of Indofrica." It used to be called "our mission in Indofrica." No one Church and no one study can possibly portray the very wide variety of growth patterns; but to see the process at work in one concrete instance will be more illuminating than to discuss it in the abstract.

I. Membership, percentage and baptisms

The most elementary information about church growth is that contained in records of church membership. So we assemble the gross membership figures for Church X from 1900 to 1950. Ideally those should be obtained for every year of the period. But for the sake of brevity we give the following round numbers for every tenth year.

Year	Membership
1900	6,000
1910	13,800
1920	17,000
1930	16,000
1940	19,900
1950	29,500

This elementary information does not tell us a great deal. However, many younger Churches and mission Boards do not look beyond it. In 1920, the supporting board of Church X, noting the increase from 13,800 to 17,000 announced cheerily, "We had a wonderful decade in Indofrica, where our Church has increased 3,200 in membership. The schools, hospitals, and agricultural settlements are flourishing and evangelism is being carried on everywhere."

This first optimistic impression is shattered when we calculate the percentage of growth for each decade. We now get a table like the following:

Year	Membership	Percentage of Church Growth Per Decade
1900	6,000	—
1910	13,800	130
1920	17,000	23
1930	16,000	—6
1940	19,900	24
1950	29,500	48

Up to this time we have discussed church growth in terms of gross increase of membership (so many hundreds or so many thousands) or have said that the membership had doubled or quadrupled or that there had been much or little growth. If we are to treat church growth seriously we must be more precise. Percentage of growth is a much better indication of church growth than gross increase and it enables much more accurate thinking than approximations such as "much growth," or "half as much again."

Since we shall use percentages again and again, those not familiar with them would do well to master the idea. Looking at the third column in the table just given, 130 means that on a membership of 6,000 in 1900 Church X, having by 1910 a gross increase of 7,800 had 130 per cent per decade church growth. The second figure—23—means that on a membership of 13,800 in 1910, Church X, having by 1920 a gross increase of 3,200, had 23 per cent per decade church growth. "—6" means that on a membership of 17,000 in 1920 Church X, having by 1930 a loss of 1,000, had a minus 6 per cent per decade church growth.

Since we are using figures from every tenth year, we automatically get percentage of church growth *per decade.* If we had used figures for three-year periods we could still readily calculate the *per decade* rate of growth of that Church. Thus, a church of 200 which grew to 260 in three years would have an average yearly increase of twenty. It would be growing at the rate of 10 per cent per annum, which is 100 per cent *per decade.*

Looking at the percentages of church growth in the table we can now see that, in a situation where church growth had been and obviously could be achieved, Church X experienced a disaster. For thirty years between 1910 and 1940 a Church which had

FIFTY YEAR GROWTH OF CHURCH X OF INDOFRICA

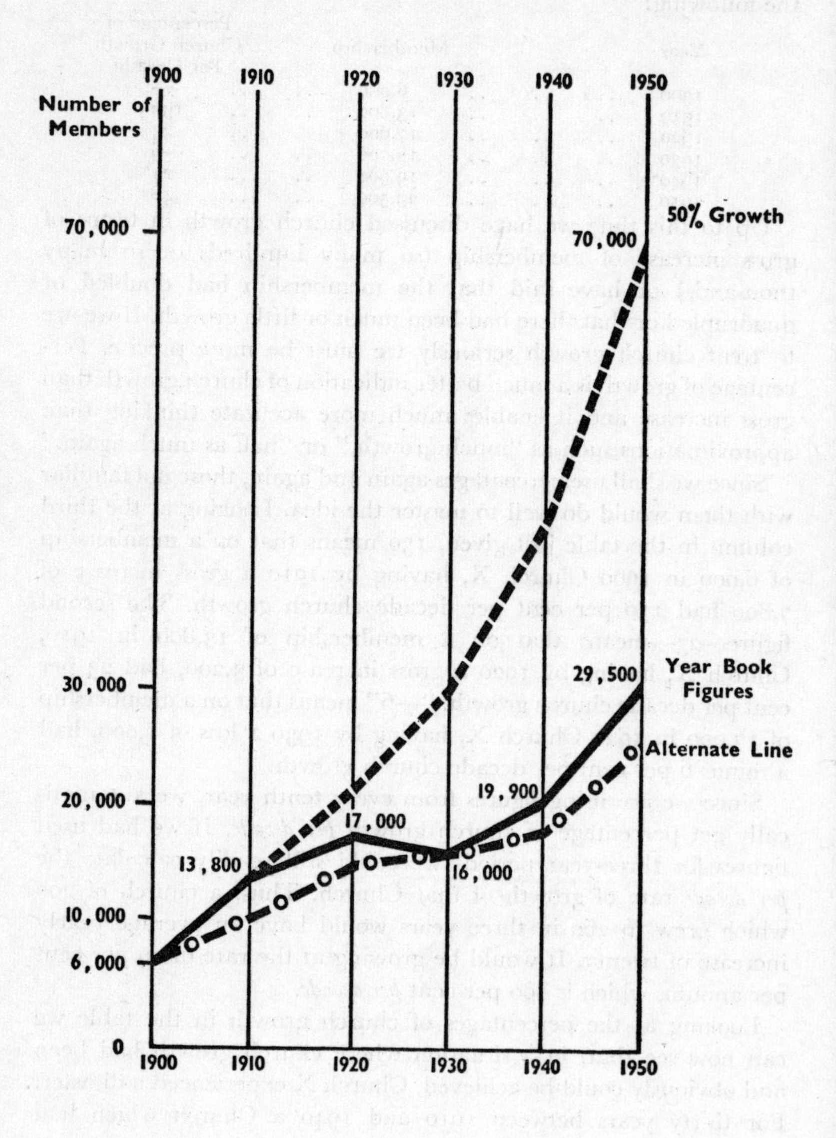

grown at 130 per cent in the previous ten years grew at an average of 13 per cent only.

We see the same picture if we make a graph of growth; it is not quite as revealing because it deals with absolute figures, not percentages. That is, looking at the solid line, the 9,600 increase of the last decade (which is only a 48 per cent increase of the membership in 1940) seems more significant than the 7,800 increase of the first decade (which is 130 per cent of the 1900 membership). Still the graph is revealing. It clearly exhibits the thirty years of disaster.

Had the supporting board been keenly aware of church growth, even this limited amount of information (figures, percentages, and graph) might have made it try to re-induce normal expansion in 1920 and 1930. It might have said, "Since we are already putting $150,000 a year into this field, let us now put in another $10,000 and find out why we are standing still." But the ministers on the board, while earnestly in favour of mission and doing all they could to inspire their congregations to greater missionary giving, looked at the small increase, charitably concluded that it was more than some of their churches had achieved, and pressed on with "splendid missions." They increased staff and budget, hopeful of growth but unaware of the structure of growth and how to achieve it. The board secretaries, missionaries and national leaders, too, saw chiefly the expansion of "the work" and rejoiced in it.

Searching for more light we investigate the record of baptisms and add them to our table. Each number of baptisms, like each percentage of growth, is for the previous ten years.

Year	Membership	Percentage of church growth	Baptisms from The Church	Baptisms from The World
1900	6,000	—		—
1910	13,800	130	2,100	7,000
1920	17,000	25	3,500	400
1930	16,000	—6	2,200	300
1940	19,900	21	3,600	1,100
1950	29,500	48	6,300	6,100

As we look at the 400, 300 and 1,100 in the fifth column we can see the cause of the disaster from 1910 to 1940. The Church almost stopped baptizing from the world. Only 1,800 persons from the world were baptized in thirty years—sixty a year. That there were 1,800 is proof that the door was open. That there were only 1,800 is proof that church growth was not being seriously sought.

This near cessation of baptisms did not embarrass the younger Church, mission, or board. In its worst decade, it had and reported 2,500 baptisms. In the thirties, with a mere 21 per cent increase, it reported 4,700 baptisms. Once a Church has a large membership the annual crop of children of the Church, coming to the age of discretion, provides for hundreds or thousands of confirmations or baptisms from the Church itself. These are of little significance for church expansion but they sound impressive, particularly when lumped with baptisms from the world and reported as "4,700 baptisms from our great field of Indofrica."

In the twenties, there were 2,500 baptisms yet the Church declined by 1,000. What does this mean? Discipline, death, reversions, and removals are the four causes of losses in membership. Assuming the statistics of Church X to be accurate, 3,500 either died, were put out of the Church, reverted to their former faith, or moved out of this Church area. Possibly discipline was too severe, or some great migration was taking place, or some wave swept the area, and the weak in faith fell away.

It is also quite possible that the statistics were not up to date. Perhaps names of those who died, moved away, reverted, or were disciplined, had for many years not been struck from the rolls; so that the actual membership in 1920 was nearer 15,000 than 17,000. Then some new leader took over the field and in 1930 resolved to make the rolls accurate. The seeming loss of this decade would then be a book-keeping affair. Small losses since 1900 were in 1930 all added up and struck off the rolls. This purging of the rolls happens in many lands. If this is the explanation in Church X then the "alternate line" of dashes and circles in the graph would represent something like the actual state of affairs during the thirty slow years. They would still show as slow years, but the dip of the twenties would be eliminated.

In the graph, the uppermost line—composed of dashes—shows what a staid 50 per cent per decade growth would have achieved. At 50 per cent Church X would have grown from 13,800 in 1910 to 20,700 to 31,050 to 46,500 to 70,000 in 1950. Such growth is no flight of fancy. It is achievable. If we compare this with what actually was achieved, then instead of rejoicing in a growth from 6,000 to 29,500 in fifty years, as we were inclined to do after a glance at the elementary information, we would sorrow that the fumblings and inadequate resources of three decades had robbed Church X of great growth.

Nowhere does "ice-age" thinking show itself more clearly than in the instant defence most churchmen make of little growth. They expect little growth. They seldom blame the board, the mission, or the younger Church. They usually believe that little growth is caused by factors beyond their control and defend it as a good thing. "After the great growth of the first decade," they say, "the mission settled down to the prosaic but more necessary work of consolidation." They might speak less kindly saying, "The careless ingathering of the first decade caused endless problems. Repeated purges were required before the Church could be called Christian. Intolerable burdens of an illiterate membership were, however, cheerfully borne and now, after three decades of sound work, we are beginning to get out of the wood."

It just might be that this description is accurate, and that there was careless over-expansion which required great skill to consolidate. But in many cases the facts are otherwise. Arrested growth is usually caused not by over-expansion but by errors in handling the resulting Church. It takes skill to perfect what has been gathered and still go on discipling. Continued discipling usually requires increased resources also. Arrested growth is seldom good mission policy. It comes about through lack of skill, or lack of resources or both. Plateaux in growth are usually made by man not ordained by God.

As we look at the record of Church X we should beware of defending it as wise churchmanship. Facts are likely to indicate that the 130 per cent of the first decade could have been continued and even accelerated had the opportunity been correctly handled.

II. Field totals and homogeneous units

So far, the membership figures we have used have been "field totals" for "our Church in Indofrica." This is common practice. When we want to know about past church growth in Congo or California, we reach for the denomination's year book, note our "total membership in each land" and compare it with what we

THE HOMOGENEOUS UNITS COMPOSING CHURCH X

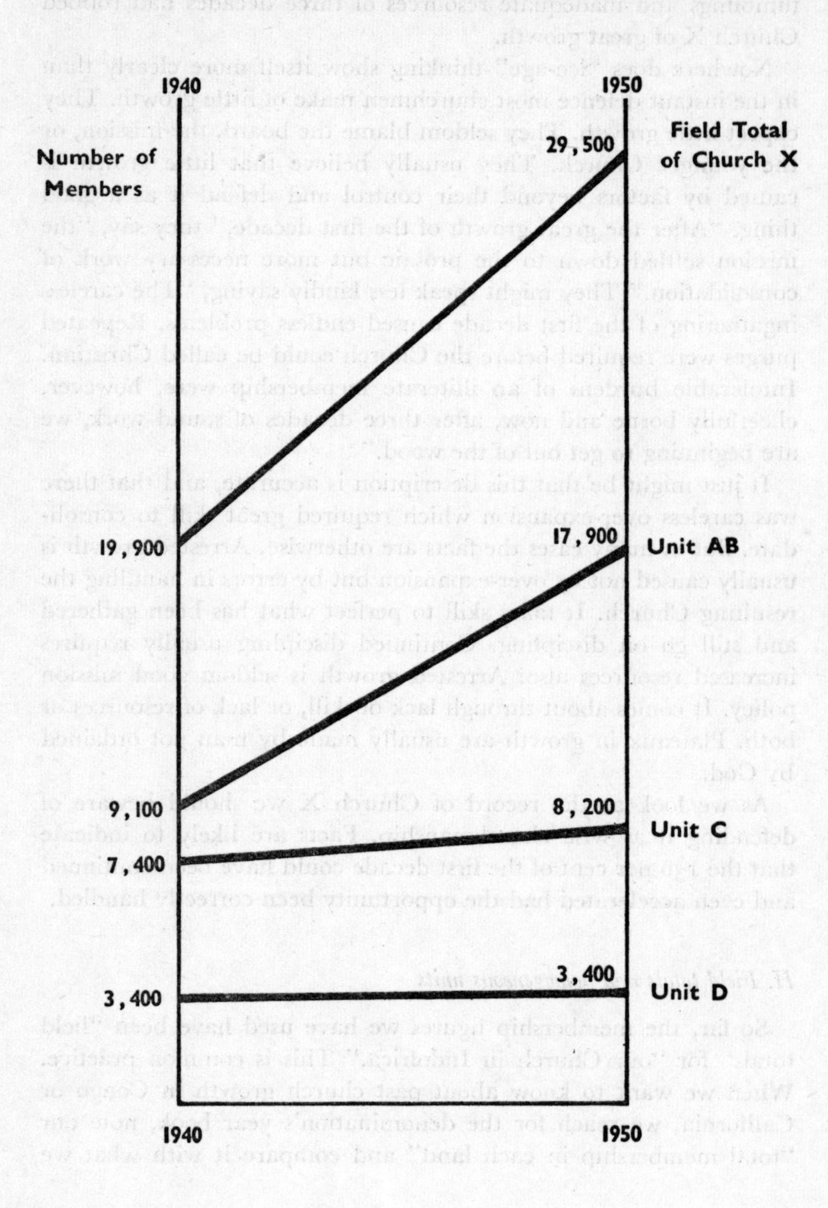

had there a year or many years ago. These "field totals," however, are figures of very limited usefulness. They conceal more than they reveal. They lump all churches into one, hide both notable advances and disastrous retreats, cancel gains against losses, and come up with figures such as we have presented. We look at these and easily draw erroneous conclusions.

For example, returning to our table, we look at the figures for one decade, 1940–1950, and say, "Well, 12,400 baptisms, nearly 10,000 increase in membership; and an over-all 48 per cent increase. Not bad. The work appears to be progressing." But let us look more deeply into the structure of church growth and we shall find how mistaken we are.

Church X (our mission in Indofrica) is composed of four stations (or areas), A, B, C and D.

Station A's membership grew from 8,400 to 15,900. Among the same people fifty miles east is Station B where the membership of 700 in 1940 is now one of 2,000. In C, where there is a different type of people, 7,400 members in 1940 grew for one year and then stood still at 8,200 for the next nine. In D, where there is a third type of people, the membership of 3,400 ten years ago is still 3,400. The field-totals printed in the Year Books are 19,900 for 1940 and 29,500 for 1950.

Since A and B are really a homogeneous unit, we shall unite their figures. The graph of growth for these three units—AB, C and D—follows.

If we look first at the "field total" line, we shall conclude that Church X is most prosperous. But if we are to understand church growth at all, we must look at the three lines below. Then we shall realize that we are really dealing with three units, AB prospering at 97 per cent and C and D not prospering at all. The accidents of geography and mission administration have tied together into "one Church" these several units. We do not have a single unit. We have three. Error in discernment here will mean error in almost every dealing with this situation; whereas understanding its multiple structure is the first step towards the correct nurture of the growing Church.

It cannot be over-emphasized that statistics, if these are to have any meaning, should be gathered by those who know the churches well and who are concerned that the statistics reveal the truth. They should also be accompanied by a full description of the churches, their natural groupings, and their geographical, social and spiritual environment. Statistics are a summary of significant information and care should be taken that they convey true meanings.

The welfare and growth of this younger Church demand not merely "a carrying on of church and mission work in our encouraging field of Indofrica," but an exact knowledge of each homogeneous unit and a tailoring of effort to fit it.

When the several units in the one package are not seen because the field total is the only figure given, it is inevitable that the missionary society send a given amount to the country, regardless of the varying degrees of growth. So much goes to Burma, so much to Ethiopia, so much to Bolivia, with the Church in each land seen as a single package, instead of what it often is—a bundle of unequally growing units.

Younger Churches also need to see the multiple structure of growth, for with them, too, the accident of administration has bound into an artificial package very different types of organisms. Often the headquarters of a mission and younger Church founded by it, for reasons of convenience in transmitting money and personnel from abroad, has been located in a port city. Should the congregations there be non-growing, a static headquarters is bound into one organization with fertile fringes. When this "one Church" has its meetings, the country cousins meet their city relations. Whose opinions and desires have greater weight is seldom in question.

Often church union brings several denominational Churches together. This will increasingly take place. Thus several packages are now regarded as "One Church." The boards, in search of more complete unity, pool their resources so that the "one Church" has one budget of assistance and one pool of missionary helpers. The Field Total of this "one Church" is now made up of the field totals of the several uniting Churches. The one over-all figure conceals variations of growth more than ever. The package is bigger *and more dangerous than ever.*

If church growth is to be achieved and stagnation avoided,

United Churches must keep in mind the homogeneous units which comprise them and must recognize that, despite a degree of interdependence, each has its own different life, and grows or declines at a different rate. Nothing is gained by glossing over these fundamental organic differences in the name of unity. On the contrary, if the United Churches are to enjoy maximum growth they must know accurately the growth history of each component unit and estimate correctly its growth potential. Then only can they act to secure great church growth.

Wise administration by Church or Mission does not consist in blanket decisions to distribute resources according to long established percentages, paying no attention to, or even being ignorant of, the structure of church growth. Wise administration insists on being furnished with accurate knowledge of the degree, quality, nature, and probable future extent of church growth in each homogeneous unit or group of congregations. It then can make such choices as to methods, personnel, and distribution of resources as will achieve maximum growth.

PART II

POPULATION FACTORS IN CHURCH GROWTH

V

HOW IS THE POPULATION COMPOSED?

To foreigners all natives look alike. To Europeans all American women seem to have been made in the same mould. An Indian going to Africa says that, despite superficial tribal differences, all Africans are one people. American commercial men in India speak as if Indians were a homogeneous population.

Ardent nationalists also, feeling that imperialists have divided and ruled them long enough, minimize interior differences. They assert that theirs is one homogeneous nation. "Friend," said an educated Yoruba of Nigeria to me, "I am not a Yoruba. I am not a Nigerian. I am an African."

The Christian Church too, labouring toward amity among the various tribes, tongues, and kindreds in its membership, is strongly inclined, disregarding the compartments in which mankind lives, to do its thinking on the lofty plane of a common humanity.

In congregations made up of those who have left their peoples in order to become Christians, one does not ask, "What tribe or caste do you belong to?" That is an insulting question. Tribe and caste have been renounced. These Christians prefer to be known by the nation to which they belong.

For these reasons the Church in its multitudinous forms is likely to think of people amongst whom it works as Chinese, Indonesians, Africans, or Indians. To the extent that it does this, it labours under an illusion—that those with whom it works are fundamentally a homogeneous population; that one person is very much like another; and that all have the same background, culture, psychology and racial characteristics.

The reality is otherwise. A nation is usually a conglomerate of peoples, sometimes bound together by language, religion and culture and sometimes divided by just these factors.

Three hundred years ago in the Philippines there were scores of tribes. These have now partly fused—unified first by Spanish civilization and later by universal education in English. Still, the major language groups remain separate—Tagalogs, Ilocanos, Tinguians, and many others.

In India within one language area are many castes: one town may have in it fifty castes. Each believes itself to be a separate people and scrupulously keeps its intimate life to itself.

In Africa a hundred years ago each tribe had its own separate territory and its own dialect or language. Today in vast rural stretches this is still true, but in urban and industrial areas men from many tribes assemble to form a partially non-tribal society. However, even those who now feel superior to their tribe usually choose their wives or daughters-in-law from their own "folk."

At first sight Thailand gives the impression of having a highly homogeneous Buddhist population. Closer examination shows that, of the population of 20 million, over 3 million are Chinese immigrants who continue to speak Swatow and consider themselves definitely a people apart. A million are Muslims. 100,000 recent immigrants are from Chinese animistic tribes. Another 100,000 are Karens. The 15 million who remain are by no means homogeneous. Those in the North are a distinct people, speaking a different kind of Thai. Even in the central plains there are various tribal strands—such as the Lao Sung—which continue a distinct existence. Then, too, once outside the highly developed urban centres, the animism of the villages is so great that one might be justified in dividing Thailanders into animists slightly washed with Buddhism and Buddhists slightly washed with animism. Thailand is a congerie of peoples.

The composition of the population is an important factor in church growth. Each people is played upon by many different forces to prevent or produce responsiveness to the Good News. If a given people is played on by a dozen forces which harden it against the Gospel, then response from its individuals will be difficult, and group conversion will be impossible. If in the same land a second people has these dozen forces playing on it to a greatly reduced degree and, in addition, has several forces bearing down on it favourable to the Gospel, then from it individual response will be relatively easy, and group conversions will become possible.

The illusion which commonly claims churchmen is that they are working with one vast crop in an illimitable plain, all parts of which are equally favoured by sun and rain. The reality is that they are working with patches of land which tilt in every direction, are in various stages of dryness and wetness, and are covered with a huge variety of crops in every stage of development. Their task is not to labour everywhere, disregarding the soil, crop, and degree of ripeness. Their task is to gather ripe sheaves into the granaries of God. This may mean some sowing and care of seedlings in various stages of development; but it must mean discerning fields ready for harvest and concentrating effort there until the last sheaf has been carried with rejoicing into God's presence.

Let us see what the composition of the population means for church growth in a specific situation. Take Puerto Rico. The many younger Churches and missions in the island are not working with "Puerto Ricans considered as a uniform kind of people." They are working with labourers in the cane fields, tobacco farmers, coffee planters, small town aristocracy, or the Roman Catholic élite of the big towns who marry back into Spain. They get a different response from every group. It is no accident that the fastest growing Church recruits largely from one stratum of society. Its type of worship, standard of ministry, and church activities fit that stratum of society.

Japan is supposed to have a homogeneous population. Castes or tribes are unknown. Education is universal. Industrialization is far advanced. Yet the clan villages compose a distinct stratum of society with a close-knit social structure. Each group of villages forms a distinct community. So different is this stratum from urban areas that so far there are extremely few churches in it. The plantings there have not yet ripened. Most churches arise in the urban areas.

However, even in the urban areas there are sub-divisions significant for church growth. One experienced churchman said of his city, "Most of our conversions take place among students, some among young married people, and very few among people over thirty-five." He was saying that the age groupings in his city had a momentous bearing on church growth. If he described a general condition, it has significance for the entire Japanese Church.

Coming to Africa we can see that a single tribe often has sub-divisions. In the eighteen-thirties among the Fanti speaking tribes of the Gold Coast there was a group which had become traders with the outside world. These resided at ports, sent their sons to learn English, occasionally journeyed by sailing ship to England, and formed an *avant garde* among their tribes. Christianity first took root in this sub-division.

Two sub-divisions existed in the Jewish community around the Mediterranean Sea. In the first were the strict racial Jews. In the second were Palestinian Jews who had themselves come to regret or question the racialism and legalism of their religion, proselytes, and sympathizers who liked the beliefs of Judaism but were held out by its laws. Among the last some had married Jews, were employed by them, or were in other ways on the fringe of the synagogue communities. Judaism took a strict line with all non-Jews. "Be circumcised," it said, "do not eat pork, observe the Sabbath, and obey all the Law strictly. Then only can you be a Jew and find favour with God."

This had been Saul's position till, illumined with the light of Christ, he saw that men might find favour with God through justification by faith and salvation by grace. When Paul arrived in a new synagogue he proclaimed Jesus as Messiah, declaring that this new dispensation was for all, and it was no longer necessary to be circumcised and bound by prohibitions not to eat this or that. His message delighted that sub-division of the synagogue community which was irked by the legalistic, racial requirements of an otherwise attractive religion. It infuriated the other sub-division—the strict racial Jews. Thus in synagogue after synagogue he won the first population and was driven out of town by the second.

Labour groupings also form sub-divisions of society. Some might have significance for church growth. Where peasants travel to some city to become factory-workers, rick-shaw pullers, miners or boatmen, leaving their wives and children behind, there the labour groups are probably not significant. The men would hesitate to become Christians without their families, and, if they did, their chance of remaining Christian, after they went back to scattered villages and had no continuing Christian nurture, would be small. But where men with families move into a centre, there the labour groupings might have significance for the spread of the Faith.

As he views the groupings, sub-divisions and strata of the population near him, the questions which every churchman, national or missionary, must ask himself are: "What plantings do I have near me? Which are ripest? Where is the unharvested crop likely to rot in the field? Where do the winds blow so as to assist winnowing? Which are the unripe plantings where the task is that of watching?"

How populations are composed is a factor of great importance for church growth. It is essential to discern each separate community and its degree of readiness.

VI

WHAT DOES EACH POPULATION BELIEVE?

Not only are there different peoples in each general population but there are also different religions to which they belong. The younger Churches are growing among peoples whose hereditary religions are something other than Christianity. Churches always grow by converting men from some other faith. Indeed, every faith grows by converting men from another system. Hinduism converted its hundreds of millions from prior faiths, drove out Buddhism, greatly diminished Jainism, and supplanted various forms of animism. Islam converted population after population in its spread. So it is with every faith, and so with Christianity.

The prior faith has a determinative effect on how fast the new religion grows. Pentecost and the rapid expansion of the Jewish Christian Church would have been impossible except out of a Judaism eagerly expecting the Messiah. The Christianization of Europe in the way it occurred would have been impossible except out of animism. The great turning of the Philippines to Roman Catholicism in the 1600s would have not occurred except for the tribal religions of the myriad Malayan peoples of that archipelago, at the particular stage of development in which those decades caught them.

Religions exist in a large variety of forms. The varieties of Christianity enshrined in the many different Churches are nothing compared with the varieties of Hinduism, Buddhism, and Shintoism. Even Islam, which has a name for unity, when it comes to actual beliefs and practices, has great variations.

The illusion of homogeneity surrounds not merely peoples but religions also. It is easy for students of any faith to believe erroneously that all its adherents hold the same doctrines. Now there are, of course, a few widely believed dogmas in every religion. For Hindus, caste is one of these—yet some Hindus belong to "A

Society to Destroy Caste." Cow-worship is another—but plenty of Hindus will sell their barren cows to the butchers, and other Hindus eat cows which have died a natural death. Buddhists believe that non-killing is the highest religion—yet in Buddhist Thailand there are large numbers of Buddhist meat-eaters. The truth is that not only is each nation an assemblage of many different peoples, but each people believes the hereditary faith in a different sense and to a differing degree.

Churchmen at work in an area should know its main religion, so that they can present the Gospel acceptably. Just as Paul, speaking to the people of the synagogue, usually introduced his message by proclaiming that the Messiah, whom Jews had been expecting, had come in the person of Jesus of Nazareth; so a churchman speaking to Hindus might present Christ as the Sinless Incarnation, or to Communists might declare that the welfare of man is a chief concern of God in Christ. Knowledge of the religion currently held by his neighbours is a valuable tool in presenting the Christian religion.

For church growth, however, the variety is at least as important as the common core of the religion believed. Many would say it is more important. There are varieties of Buddhists, Hindus, Muslims and Communists, numbering in some cases thousands and in others millions, who are approachable. There are others who—at this time and under these circumstances—have, to use a biblical way of speaking, had their hearts hardened so that they may not believe. To work out a statement of the Gospel acceptable to Hindus is not so much needed as to work out a statement acceptable to those varieties of Hindus who are showing themselves approachable. To preach the Gospel ardently to all Shintoists is not so much needed as to preach it ardently to those groupings which are responsive.

There is no merit in selecting the least responsive people to preach to. Yet the exploratory phase of the world mission of the Church has left a large number of missions and small non-growing churches in the midst of "unripe" varieties of Muslims, Hindus, and Shintoists who, far from welcoming Christian evangelism, resent it; and far from yielding a steady stream of churches, fight the establishment of even one. These stations and churches say, "Anyone can labour in the easy fields where converts can be won and churches established. It takes real Christians to work the hard fields such as ours." It is almost as if they said, "The only real Shintoists are those who reject the Gospel. Real Christians are those who present Christianity to these Gospel-rejecting Shintoists!"

On the contrary, once the concept of varieties within each faith has gripped the mind of a churchman, he realizes that there is no merit in calling only those real religionists who reject Christianity. Those Buddhists, for example, who accept Christianity are as real Buddhists as those of a somewhat different stamp who reject it, and *they are much more important for church growth.* Had Paul presented the Gospel solely to the "real" Jews or the "real" Gentiles, he would have met little response. Instead he presented it to those Jews and Gentiles who accepted it, or as he says, "turned to God" or were "called to be saints." They were the ones who made the New Testament Church possible.

Instead therefore of a study of Buddhism, Hinduism, or Islam, being made on a basis which treats each religion as a unit, schools of missionary preparation and theological seminaries of the younger Churches need to teach the faiths of mankind, attending specially to those varieties which respond to Christian teaching. What in the Confucianism of district Y makes Confucianists there turn to the Christian faith? That is the comparative religion of importance for Christians. It is almost entirely a virgin field.

In addition to the great faiths there is also animism, both in its pure and modified form. The pure animist believes that things seen, like animals, trees, rivers, rocks, mountains, fields, and diseases, have spirits or personalities which can be pleased or enraged and who cause all the sorrows which man is heir to. Animism usually has no book. The spirits it placates vary from locality to locality. It is the universal religion of primitive mankind. It was the first religion of Europeans.

When man emerges into civilization, he usually accepts some higher religion in a nominal or group fashion while his real belief continues in the spirits. This mixed belief is modified animism. Thus Buddhists in vast stretches of rural Asia are scarcely real Buddhists. They are modified animists. Popular Hinduism, the religion of the masses in India, gives ten times as much money for the placation of the evil spirits as it does for the worship of the gods of the Hindu scriptures. While Hinduism stresses the sanctity of animal life, scores of millions of Hindus *as their real religion* daily sacrifice goats, roosters, pigs, or other animals to local deities or vengeful spirits. They are not as much Hindus as modified animists.

A letter from a colleague lies before me:

> A cholera epidemic raged in Pata village last week. About a fifth of the men of the village are literate. Its chief man is a college graduate. No one has yet become Christian. The epidemic was stopped by injections given by the mission doctor. After it had been stopped, the village council decided to discover who had brought in the cholera spirit. They taxed each house a measure of grain to provide funds to call the magicians for the trial. After an intensely vivid procedure, which must have burned belief in evil spirits into the consciousness of every child, they declared a certain woman guilty and sentenced her to be driven out of the village.

Examples could be given from every land. This is not residual animism, such as is displayed in advanced societies east and west in, for example, a half fanciful shunning of the number thirteen. This is a serious major belief which continues, generation after generation.

Pure animism has great importance for church growth. Within the present century the progress of the world will bring all primitive or animistic people into some advanced religion. They will become Evangelical Christians, Roman Catholics, Muslims, Hindus, Buddhists, or Communists. In many areas, as a result of a hundred years of mission, the primitive peoples are inclined to Christian faith; yet the pressures of nationality and contiguous cultures will push them into other faiths, unless Christendom accelerates and intensifies her efforts to win them.

The force of this most significant fact, however, has been greatly mitigated by the prejudiced racial assumption that animistic peoples did not count. It was believed that they were biologically inferior human stock, and hence were primitive. Thus animistic Karens were supposed to have less brains than Buddhistic Burmans (actually racially their first cousins and physically indistinguishable from them!). The Muslim Fulani of north Nigeria were judged superior human material compared with the animist Ibo of south Nigeria, though only two centuries ago they must have been very much alike indeed.

This thinking, far from being confined to westerners, has been even more characteristic of converts from the "superior" races of the non-Occident. For example, often "upper caste" Christians are scornful of church work among the "backward races" of India.

Happily much racial thinking of both westerners and nationals is rapidly giving way to a truer evaluation. It is seen that the depressed animists of today, given opportunity, are the solid citizens of tomorrow. Primitives who become Christians do not remain primitives. Tribal peoples in India who become Christians will unquestionably become solid citizens with their due share of great men. The animists of northern Nigeria are going to be the educated voters of that land, either as Muslims or Christians.

If pure animists, who can be won today, are spurned by Christians seeking to win irresponsive Muslims, Buddhists, or Hindus, then in the next forty years these animists will become Muslims, Buddhists or Hindus.

For church growth, modified animism, too, is highly significant. Fully half of all response to the Gospel in India has come from modified animists. The strength of the Church in Burma has come from modified animists. The Muslims who by the hundreds are embracing Christianity in Africa are modified animists. Furthermore, as Christianity in all lands begins to multiply after these past decades of exploration and probing, it is highly probable that it will grow most rapidly among the hundreds of millions who are now listed as Confucianists, Shintoists, Buddhists or Hindus, but whose real inner belief is the placation of the evil spirits.

Churchmen who work among modified animists must know the actual religion of those whom they serve. What is really believed? For what is money spent? In what kind of worship do the people actually take part? Books may not be available. The likelihood that a book has been written on the actual religion of the specific people with whom a given churchman works is not great. But observation and inquiry, particularly from converts, can readily be made.

The modified animism of greatest significance for church growth is that from which there is response to the Christian message. Once churches start to be established, there is great need for careful description of the particular variety of modified animism from which the churches arise.

For example, in a Buddhist land, the population of a certain district was found to be responsive. The churches were doubled in a decade without special reinforcement. The bishop of the district—a national—ascribed the great growth chiefly to the fact that his churches were composed of Christians who sincerely believed in evil spirits, but also believed that the Lord Jesus Christ has power over evil spirits. Christians did not ridicule the modified animism of their neighbours, nor, considering them Buddhists, preach to them "a Gospel suitable for Buddhists." They merely proclaimed, more by their lives than word of mouth, that Christ was more powerful than evil spirits, that prayer to God was more effective than incense and sacrifice, and that evil spirits did not trouble Christians. This kind of Saviour appealed to these modified animists. Many became Christians.

Interestingly enough, the western trained churchmen assisting that growing Church, expressing a scientific frame of mind, today deplore what they call "this magic in reverse." They feel the pastors should educate the Christians to recognize that evil spirits do not exist. If the western party succeeds in pushing the pastors into such educational efforts, church growth from among those country people will stop. The approach of science—that there are no evil spirits—will be adopted. The approach of faith—that there are evil spirits but the Lord can control them—which has won conversions from the pre-scientific, modified animists will be discarded.

Finally, in the whole area of "what the people believe," the Churches must come to terms with a major element—the nominal of all faiths. Not only are there people which are correctly labelled Animists, Hindus, Muslims, and others; and not only are there hosts of smaller people each believing some special variety of the main religion, but in each variety of each religion there are the practising members and the nominal members.

Some devout laymen were discussing the Church in America. It was their general opinion that less than one in three members were "born-again Christians." Some estimated the proportion as low as one in ten. If this is true in the West, where the Churches for scores of years have engaged in a tremendous programme of Christian education, we may be sure that of the millions whom we carelessly term Muslims, Confucianists, or Hindus, much larger numbers know nothing about their religion, have never read their own scriptures, nor have any intention of bringing their personal conduct into harmony with them. They are Confucianists, Buddhists, or what not, merely in name. There are hundreds of millions of them.

What is the significance for church growth of this tremendous number of religionists merely in name? First, it underlines the need of conversion—of active personal acceptance of Christ. "Nominals," by the standards of their own religion, to say nothing of Christianity, are without God and without hope in the world. They will remain so, until they are individually converted.

Second, this state of affairs means that the witness to Christ must have a knowledge of the other man's actual religion, not "according to the book," but to the "haphazard bundle" of what is actually believed and practised. This bundle does have a certain undefined relationship to the accepted religious systems. In a general way it stems from it, but it has also departed a long way from it. The nominal adherent is not moved by theological niceties: he is moved by much more practical considerations. It is in this elastic area that the witness to Christ needs knowledge.

Third, this large number of nominal believers gives great hope that people are not nearly as fixed in other moulds as we think. There are hundreds of millions who are Muslims, Hindus, Confucianists, and Buddhists only in the sense that logs in a boom are parts of a system. Once what holds them is gone, they will be available for rearrangement. The fact that this is also true of large numbers of Christians emphasizes the key significance of "nominalism" as a universal factor in church growth.

The battle for men's minds is being carried on by relatively small armies in the midst of countrysides full of non-combatants. The coming decades will see enormous accessions from the "nominals" to other faiths. The "great religions" will have a very different distribution as the process takes place.

VII

HOW CAN THE RESPONSIVE BE FORMED INTO CHURCHES?

We must now ask what are the characteristics which, in a responsive people, fairly well determine whether a satisfactory Church will result or not.

(1) Here is a younger Church which adds each year several hundred converts from the world. Its community is obviously responsive. With few exceptions these converts are unmarried students or ex-students. They are influenced by Christian schools, correspondence courses, and radio programmes. They live scattered out across a city and its environs. Most of their parents are not Christian, though a few have one parent who is a Christian. At the time of their conversion few are earning any money. What does this kind of situation mean for solid church growth, implying both evangelistic potency and self-support?

Since student converts are not earning, they bring little increase of income to the churches. By the time they begin earning they have been Christians for several years—Christians who have given little to the Church! They marry back into the social stratum to which they belong. The chances of their marrying Christians are not great, so families are established in which one partner is a Christian and the other is not. Because of this many gradually quit coming to church. Since they live across the city, and often move from one section to another, the chance of their forming permanent associations in congregations is not high. Congregations of these converts tend to be made up of those whose chief bond of association is their faith. Residence, business, family, friends, tend to throw them with non-Christians. Furthermore, most converts have come into the church as the result of long study in school. They have little experience of conversion being caused by the witness and worship of individuals and small groups. So they expect that the way to become Christian is through long education in Christian schools.

With these characteristics, the chances of great church growth are low. These hundreds of unmarried student converts are a good beginning, but before great church growth can be hoped for, earning families must be won, and a mode of ingathering, independent of the school, must be worked out.

(2) Here is a responsive caste from which both individuals and groups are constantly being baptized, but it is a scattered caste with only two or three families to a village. It is an oppressed backward population, and none of the other castes resident in these villages are accepting Christ. When a hundred families of the responsive people have become Christian, the resulting congregation spreads over 2,000 square miles of territory in fifty villages. It cannot get together for weekly worship. The pastor, to support whom a congregation of about a hundred families is needed, must visit on foot all fifty villages to see his flock. Here, though the community is highly responsive, its wide dispersion makes the establishment of self-supporting self-propagating congregations difficult.

By contrast, a responsive community with fifty families to a village, furnishes an excellent opportunity for church establishment.

(3) The economic potential of the responsive population is also important for the growth of the Church. Observe three great communities. First, all through south-east Asia are the Chinese of the dispersion—3 million in Thailand, a million or more in Indonesia, scores of thousands in the Philippines and Burma, thousands in India, and very large numbers in Indo-China. These are energetic, resourceful, hardworking, and intelligent people. Many of them are merchants. Almost the whole business of Indonesia is in Chinese hands. Even in far-off Jamaica many shop-keepers are Chinese. Second, there are the landless depressed classes of south India, where the Untouchables, from whom the Church has largely come, have from time immemorial been essentially serfs. Perhaps one in ten now owns an acre or two of land. Third, there are the landed tribes of Burma, Africa, and Indonesia, where individuals commonly own from two to fifty acres of land. The chances of church growth, out beyond the mothering care of some mission, are different in each of these peoples by virtue of the economic factor alone.

(4) Consider also "whole people" Churches *versus* conglomerate Churches. Here is a people all of whose members speak the same dialect, have the same traditions, intermarry with each other, have much the same occupation and level of culture. When this people becomes Christian the resulting Church has high stability, and its social structure gives endurance to its Church. Moreover, church growth is likely to be great. Conglomerate Churches, on the other hand, where the membership feels no bond of kinship, tend to be slow growing, despite any degree of spiritual excellence.

(5) Finally, here are Churches which, when discipling of the responsive segment of society is complete, will have taken in the total population of that section, and here are others which, when discipling of the segment is complete, will have taken in only 5 per cent of the total population. For the establishment of the Church the first is much more significant.

PART III

GENERAL FACTORS IN CHURCH GROWTH

VIII

AUTHENTIC SPIRITUAL FIRE

We have described certain human factors in church growth. We shall go on to describe others. But we are not describing a human enterprise. The redemption of the world is the chief concern of God. This is the central doctrine in the Christian religion. This is what the incarnation was to achieve. This was the purpose of the Cross. The great Commission, comprising the last words of Christ during His earthly ministry, describes what must be done if the purposes of God in Christ are carried out.

The growth of the Church is always brought about by the action of the Holy Spirit. As in the New Testament Church, so today, the Holy Spirit leads, convicts of sin, converts, builds up, selects missionaries and thrusts them out to ripened fields. The concern of Christians today must be to understand the workings of the Holy Spirit and to be open to His leading. We talk of factors producing readiness to accept the Saviour—but who produces the factors? It is largely the Holy Spirit of God. We but describe the way in which He acts. He upbuilds the Church, extends and nurtures it. Men are the channel through which He works.

It is an exhilarating thought that every effort which multiplies the Church is in the will of God. He rejoices when the Water of Life flows wide, deep, and fast to parched mankind. It is a solemn thought that failure to understand how God extends His Church, a failure heightened subtly at times by man's self-will, pride, and ignorance, can delay or prevent the gathering of all mankind into the Church.

The spiritual character of church growth is clear. We do not wish to labour the point. We are writing for fellow Christians. But we mention it lest, as we enumerate the statistical outward forms of God's action, any think that we believe church growth results from merely human efforts.

Radiant personal faith on the part of younger and older Churches, ministers and missionaries, laymen and youth, is an irreplaceable factor. Everything else can be there, but if this is absent, church growth scarcely ever occurs. Conversely, when there is authentic spiritual fire all kinds of difficult circumstances are surmounted.

In practically every land of the world are Christian communities in intimate relationship with non-Christian. Korea, Japan, Formosa, the Philippines, Thailand, Indonesia, sections of India and Africa, to mention only a few countries, have Christian communities intertwined with non-Christian in every human relationship. All new converts have relatives in the other faith. There is some intermarriage between followers of the faiths. As Christians seek work they often scatter to where there is no Church. Christian children grow up amidst non-Christians. Sons of Christian mothers and non-Christian fathers are potential Timothies. Relationship, friendship, and business bridge gulfs on every hand.

Bridges—intimate relationships—are open at both ends and on them Christians and non-Christians are engaged in a ceaseless, even if often unconscious, tug-of-war. The more fervent have the better chances of winning. A fervent and unquestioning—though not unreasonable—conviction is the desideratum. Indeed, provided there is a bridge, the growth of the Church is, one way or another, based on fervency.

In a certain Buddhist land, for example, young people become Christian while their parents remain Buddhists. Christians marry Buddhists without exciting much comment in either community. They live in close contact with Buddhist neighbours and relatives. Does church growth take place over all these bridges? The answer for any one bridge depends on whether the Christians on it have fervent faith. In the actual situation referred to, some churches are growing, others are declining. Churches without conversion growth either have no bridges or—having them—lack radiant faith.

Fervency, however, is not the sole factor. If the church at Antioch had not channelled resources to the ripe synagogue communities of Cyprus, Pamphylia, and Pisidia, its fervency alone would not have placed congregations there. Fervent faith is like sunshine. Without it crops can't grow. With it—*and* rain, good soil, and skilful farming—crops grow abundantly.

The presence of fervent faith is marked by the presence and power of the Holy Spirit and the manifest blessing of God. A Church may have all the factors which lead to fruitfulness, yet, not seeking the blessing of God, remain barren. Prayer for spiritual infilling has again and again played an important part in the growth of the Church. It was influential in the great growth of the Methodist Church in the Gold Coast in 1850 to 1854 and again in 1872 to 1875. Andrew Gordon, the United Presbyterian, in writing of tremendous growth in the Church in the Punjab says, "Overwhelmed with awe, lest by unwise interference on our part, we should stay the blessing of God by initiating some merely human work in place of the divine, we could but cry to the Master for the promised wisdom and earnest labourers necessary for the momentous occasion." Churches which grow are Churches which seek earnestly the gracious power of God.

However, we cannot bend God to our will. Younger Church ministers and their assisting missionaries who for any reason retire from fields where churches are multiplying to the "more important tasks" where God is not causing increase of the congregations, should not expect that their ardent prayers will cause God to transfer His power to where they choose to live.

Spiritual power often manifests itself also in a spirit of forgiveness and loving service. The husband is won when the Christian wife forgives him for a tirade or a beating. The student is won by his teacher's patience. Conversions multiply when men see Him, Who went about doing good, among them again in Christian neighbours and churches. Sometimes a Christward move has started when some population became convinced through loving service that Christianity was the true faith.

Finally, the basic beliefs of churchmen as they carry out the world mission of the Church are weighty spiritual factors in the process of church growth.

Do churchmen believe that the nature of God demands missions and church expansion? Are they sure that the source of the missionary enterprise is God Himself? Do they believe that communion with God fills us with a passion for the salvation of the world and that any communion which does not have this effect is incomplete? Does their theology affirm that God through the Holy Spirit retains the missionary enterprise in His own hands and continues as its final and only Authority?

Do churchmen believe in the uniqueness of Christ? Many evidences indicate that as nations draw closer together, not merely in space and time, but more significantly in mind and spirit, syncretism of religions will become more and more attractive. Christian missions will be tempted to become less and less the proclamation of a unique Saviour. What churchmen believe about Christ is crucial. Do they really believe Him when He says, "no man cometh unto the Father but by me"?

As physical life becomes more abundant and the comforts of a higher standard of living become more apparent, what churchmen believe about the abundant life promised by our Lord becomes increasingly important for church growth. Are they preaching the Gospel of the full dinner-pail or of reconciliation to God? Should the Church's chief effort be that men, before they have any knowledge of Christ, get plenty to eat? Or should it be first to reconcile them with God? What way, do churchmen believe, is truly best for man?

Church growth depends on winning converts. Churches grow from nothing but converts—people who believe on Jesus Christ intensely enough to break with their past sins and cleave to Him as Lord and Saviour. Converts are not picked up lying loose on the beach. They are won by men and women whose own beliefs blaze hot enough to kindle faith in others. This involves the conviction that it is truly better for a man to leave father and mother and sister and brother, if need be, to obtain Christ. Church growth occurs more readily where churchmen believe that it makes an eternal difference whether one is a Christian or not and whether one's community is Christian or not.

There is a definite relationship between the intensity of belief, often expressed in absoluteness and exclusiveness, and the rate of growth. This is a factor which works in favour of Churches like the Roman Catholic and others which believe that they are the only true Church.

Sometimes Churches develop ability to co-operate at the cost of intensity of belief. Indeed, belief that "our position is the only right one" is incompatible with friendly co-operation with other Churches. In order to co-operate with Churches holding somewhat different doctrines, Churches surrender belief in the absolute rightness of some of their positions. Just how far can this surrendering go?

Co-operating Churches must make sure that, while granting freedom to other Churches on matters of opinion, they maintain absolute faith in the essentials, and that they do not extend the ecumenical mind (correct between various Branches of the one Church of Christ) to the radically different religions of the world where it becomes the equivalent of syncretism.

As other factors in church growth come under study, these spiritual forces should be borne in mind. They are of extreme importance.

IX

WHAT DO THE SCRIPTURES SAY OF MISSION?

Many Christians today, seeking an irenic mode of evangelism, define mission not as winning men to Christ, but merely as witnessing to Him by word or, better, by deed and life. They quietly demonstrate the redeemed life—goodness, kindness, brotherhood, and peace. Their goal is not persuading men to become disciples of Christ. Their duty, they believe, is complete when they have lived as Christians. They do not aim for church growth or, in the slightest degree, measure success by whether men do in fact accept Jesus Christ as Lord and Saviour.

Is this view of "mission" correct? Is mission rightly defined as such witness? Do the Scriptures uphold this view? What do they say as to the nature of mission, its central objective and its continuing end?

(1) *The unequivocalness of mission*

In the New Testament, mission is proclamation or witness of a life or death message. Those who believe the message will be saved: those who reject it will be lost. The Church observed that many believed and many did not. Those who did not remained out of Christ. This was observable fact. They were outside the channel of salvation. John's Gospel, chapter 3, says, "He who will not believe is sentenced already. . . . He that believeth not the same shall not see life, but God's wrath abides on him." This inexorable aspect is integral to New Testament mission. It made Christianity a laughing stock among the intelligentsia of the Empire—and gave it a cutting edge which eventually convinced them. Unequivocal certainty underlies Acts 4: 12, Romans 5: 17, Mark 16: 15 and many other passages.

For Luke, certainty manifests itself in witness of a deliberately planned and clearly foretold salvation. In Luke 24: 44 our Lord says, "When I was with you, I told you that whatever is written about me in the law of Moses and the prophets and the psalms must be fulfilled. . . . Thus it is written that the Christ had to suffer and on the third day rise from the dead, and that repentance and forgiveness of sins should be preached in His name to all nations. . . . You are witnesses of these things." In Acts 1: 8, He says, "You shall be my witnesses in Jerusalem and in all Judea and Samaria and to the end of the earth." Disciples were to bear testimony that Jesus' death and resurrection were not forced or accidental, but were according to the eternal purposes of God, foretold in the Scriptures, had really taken place, and hence "there is salvation in no one else."

(2) *The universality of mission*

In the New Testament, mission is universal. The meaning of Christ's whole life, teachings, death, and resurrection is universal salvation. "Everyone who acknowledges me before men, I will acknowledge before my Father. . . . No one knows the Son except the Father and no one knows the Father except the Son and him to whom. . . . I am the light of the world. . . . I am the bread of life, if anyone eats of this bread. . . . I am the door, if anyone enters by me. . . ." Many other passages come at once to mind. True, disciples of the first few years, chained by Jewish concepts and customs, "spake the word to none but Jews"; but the universal gospel could not be confined. It broke both racial exclusiveness and legalistic theology to establish Christianity as available by faith to all tribes, tongues, kindreds and nations. Hence the Gospel was for all men. Mission was to all people bar none.

(3) *The urgency of mission*

In the New Testament, mission was to be before the end came. When we ponder Christ's words in Matthew 24: 14 we understand more of what mission meant to the early Church. "This gospel of the kingdom shall be preached in all the world for a witness to all peoples (tribes, clans, castes, kindreds) and then shall the end come." Mission to the early churches was persuading men to accept the Gospel *before the day of judgment came*. Romans 9–11 shows mission in relation to the coming end more clearly than most other passages. The intervening days, however long they proved to be, were a time of grace during which all who believed would be saved.

From the beginning, the Christians at Jerusalem held this true for all Jews. Part of their missionary zeal rose from their determination to win their loved ones before the days of grace ran out. As the universality of Christianity (gradually becoming visible in the successive disciplings of the Samaritans, the household of Cornelius, the Greeks at Antioch, and then around the Great Sea) broke upon Christians, some of them ejaculated simply: "So God has actually allowed the Gentiles to repent and live!" (Acts 11: 18). Others came to a complicated formula like that of Paul (Romans 9–11) in which he judges that the stubborn rejection of Christ by a great body of the Jews was only a partial insensibility "till the full number of the Gentiles" had come in. This done, "All Israel will be saved, as it is written." All Christians, both those at Jerusalem and around the Empire, would have said that mission continued so that in the days of grace men and women, Jews and Gentiles, as they believed, might be saved.

(4) *The passion of mission*

In the New Testament, mission meant a passion to save. Andrew goes at once and finds his brother. Paul in Corinth argues daily in the synagogue persuading Jews, with preaching and testifying, that Jesus is the Christ. Later Paul writes to these Corinthians that his life-work is to beseech them to be reconciled to God. He vigorously maintains that he has been all things to all men, so that he might by all means save some. He even goes so far as to wish himself "accursed and cut off from Christ" if only more of his fellow Jews could be saved. Tens of thousands had been saved, but he wanted more and more.

The Great Commission of our Lord, in the final verses of Matthew's Gospel, unite these four—unequivocalness, universality, urgency, and passion—into a full statement of New Testament Mission. If this definitive saying of the Lord Jesus had been lost, it could be re-created today because it describes so accurately what the New Testament Church did—i.e. what Mission was to the Early Church.

Proclamation and witness were consummated in "making disciples of." That is what they were intended for. Good News was to be proclaimed to every creature *so that* he might become a disciple. Christians were to bear testimony to the life, death, and resurrection of Christ, *so that*, before the end, all tribes might become disciples of Christ. In short, Mission was—through proclamation of God's mighty acts and fervent witness to what "we have seen and heard"—*inducing all men and women to become disciples of Christ and learn what He had commanded.*

Mission in the New Testament was never proclamation for proclamation's sake, never simply living as Christians, indifferent to whether men obeyed or not. According to the record, the passion that was God's for the salvation of mankind, of which the Cross is the supreme expression, was not shown in detached witness, or a kindly living out of the Gospel, hoping that sinful men would notice the Christian's life and seek its Source. It was never simply discharging a duty to witness. It focused not on what Christians should do, but on saving men. It was witness and proclamation, that men might believe.

Hence, it was also witness where men would become disciples. This was true during the first fifteen years, when with few exceptions, the disciples "spake the word to none but Jews." A racial and linguistic limitation operated here, to be sure; but so did a driving concern that men believe. As long as we can win multitudes of Jews, why go to the Gentiles? This was also true of Paul. He, acutely conscious of being the apostle to the Gentiles, always started with the Jews. He went to winnable people. The record tells over and over again of his beginning with the synagogue community. Even in Ephesus, where so many were converted that the idol makers were frightened, the churches started with twelve Jewish disciples, and Paul for three months confined himself to the one synagogue, "speaking out fearlessly, arguing and persuading people about the kingdom of God."

Who came to that one synagogue? How many could sit in it? Who were concerned about the exclusively Jewish concept of the kingdom of God? The answers to these questions indicate that for many months Paul preached to a relatively small number of Jews, proselytes, and near proselytes. These again were split into the racially liberal and the racially conservative. The first party must have constituted a majority in that synagogue—or Paul could not have remained in it for three months. But as more and more Gentiles were drawn in—but not more than the place would seat—the racially conservative Jews, dismayed at the presence of these repugnant outsiders, fought against and derided Paul. So he withdrew to the School of Tyrannus taking with him over half of the synagogue community—a fairly small number. Again Paul had started in the synagogue where men could be won. Again he had shifted out of that, when no more could be won there, to go to a new ripe field—those Gentiles who were in intimate connection with the new disciples of Christ. Again and again we see the Church shifting out of reaped fields into new ripe fields—out of Jerusalem into Antioch, out of Antioch into Pisidia, out of the reaped synagogue into the school of Tyrannus.

The Church went *where men could be won* and there witnessed and preached the Word *that men might believe, become disciples, form churches of Christ, and be found in them at the end.* Proclamation and witness were means to discipling. Mission meant winning men for Christ and organizing them into churches, that they in turn might disciple more men and organize more churches. This is the plain evidence of the New Testament.

Today there is acute theological concern about the relationship of mission to results. What the Scriptures say of mission and what the Early Church did in mission casts clear light here. The theological issue is germane to the conduct of missions in this rapidly changing world situation; and is well stated in the following sentences from Dr. Kraemer's superb summary of the world and mission in *The Christian Message in a Non-Christian World:*

> The Kingdom is a reality that works already in many manifest and latent ways in the community of Christ but can never be the direct object and achievement of our labours, because it is in the hand of the Father. The vision of it and the actual participation in it through the ever-active work of the Holy Spirit inspire men to go out into the world to claim it for Christ and His divine, saving, and regenerating order of life; but if the claim is ignored, the messenger is not disillusioned or broken, but goes on indefatigably, loyal to his prime duty to be God's obedient servant, whether

there are results or not. Of course, he is fully alive to the importance of "success" or "results," but neither successes nor the realization of self-defined programmes are the standard for his missionary perseverance. This standard is only the apostolic obligation toward God and the world.

At first glance Dr. Kraemer's position seems diametrically opposed to our exposition of the New Testament; but really it is the same. We agree that mission recorded in the New Testament was not a "self-defined programme" carried out for "results"—either the Christianization of the social order or the increase of Christians. We agree that therefore it should not be such today. We engage in mission basically because we are part of God's Church. He indwells and directs the Church and thrusts out its members into mission—His mission. The Holy Spirit inspires Christians to mission, i.e. "to go out into the world to claim it for Christ and His divine, saving, and regenerating order of life." As Christians directed by God, we shall go where He sends us and present Christ's claims there, just because He sends us. We shall stay there as long as He keeps us there.

But this stand did not lead Barnabas and Peter and Paul, and it will not lead us, into the following paths:

(*a*) A detached neutral witness, in which we disclaim in advance any interest in results, any concern that men should accept Christ, explaining that we are merely telling the Good News of God, not persuading men to surrender to Christ. Such indifference is the antithesis of biblical mission. Conviction that the mission is God's not ours cannot lead to an indifference as to whether men, multitudes of men, believe in Christ or not. It cannot lead us to accept with equal joy as the outcome of our witness 100 or ten or one or no believer at all.

(*b*) A substitution of "the kindly service of men whatever they choose to believe" for biblical "mission." Discerning the danger of self-deception, we shall fear to avoid the offence of the Cross.

(*c*) A deliberate choice of fields where men cannot be won, while neglecting those where they can. The apostles and disciples never did this. In the vastly different conditions today men and women might well still ask themselves whether God has really sent them to areas where there is no response at all. When our Lord's pierced hand points out harvest fields, white with multitudes who can be won for Him, what justification can we give if we choose to go somewhere else?

Because "our standard is only the apostolic obligation toward God and the world" we shall go out "to claim the world for Christ and His divine saving and regenerating order of life." The inescapable obligation will be with us according to the resources and time God gives us.

Reinhold Niebuhr says that, facing immoral society, the Christian must act in the light of both the law of love and the genuine possibilities for action. In the same way, when facing men without Christ, the Christian must witness in the light both of his own redemption, his gratitude to God, his God-directedness *and* the genuine possibilities for persuasion.

In God's good purpose, many people today are ripe for the harvest. His evident intention is that white fields should be reaped. In this kind of a world God will constrain His servants to reap the harvest. The same Holy Spirit who inspires men to claim the world for Christ, also inspires them to concentrate their efforts on those areas where men are gladly coming to the Saviour.

X

CURRENT PHILOSOPHIES OF MISSIONS

An arrangement of convictions or theories about "what mission correctly is" we call a philosophy of missions. Everyone has one, whether formulated or simply a mass of judgements and habits which help determine his course of action in any given situation. Philosophies of missions have great bearing on church growth. This is particularly true today because of the varied nature of missions and the increasing spread of different conscious and unconscious philosophies of mission.

"Mission" today covers a multitude of commendable activities carried on by Christians. As the world grows smaller, travel between areas becomes quicker, and greater degrees of health, education, nutrition, and leisure are achieved by nation after nation, Christians see opportunities for numberless mission activities and start them everywhere. Churches and Missions, however, seldom trouble to discover whether their activities produce the maximum possible benefit to the Churches. Indeed, it is difficult to judge this, because what is considered beneficial depends on greatly varying philosophies of what mission essentially is.

The spread of modern mission activities is enormous. A recent writer maintains that the one great achievement of missions during the past century was the elimination of the slave trade. Another praises it as a most significant factor in the creation of world friendship. Still another berates it for not getting ahead fast enough with its main task—the establishment of full brotherhood among men. Much money flows into mission board coffers in the hope that missions will help stop Communism. A recent book says that since Asia is in revolution, Christianity should be commended to the Asian masses as the most truly revolutionary religion of all. Large missions are organized for the one purpose of preaching for a witness to all men before the coming of the Lord. Truly a tremendous spread!

Since each main type of mission activity generates a supporting theory, there are many theories of missions. These are seldom described. It is current practice to rejoice in them all and count them all as "Parts of the world mission of the Church, as broad as human need." Often they come on the stage, not in a supporting role, but as principals. Each theory feels itself to be a sufficient "end" of missions. Few of their protagonists would search the New Testament for a valid theory of missions. Our exposition in the previous chapter might appeal to them as interesting; but not decisive for today. What "mission" is, they would say, depends on the current situation in the light of our judgement as Christians.

Since we are considering factors which produce church growth and mission, these varying theories of mission are of vital interest to us.

Some theories of mission produce climates favourable to and others hostile to church growth. Some intend to achieve the growth of the churches. Others care little about this. Some intelligently work that churches may multiply; others work for other ends. Let us describe six main theories and note the part each plays in the growth of the Church.

One common theory of mission, particularly in America, considers it "service in the name of Christ to needy people." The parables of the Last Judgement, the Good Samaritan, and other texts give it a scriptural base. *A Theology of Christian Missions* was written in 1937 to support this theory. The most common objection to missions—that we have plenty of poor here without going halfway around the world to find them—considers missions a charity. Missions from wealthy nations to poor nations, inevitably overflowing in good deeds, help to create this theory of missions. In fields where there is much opposition and little church growth, the good deeds done in Christ's name comprise a very large part of the total Christian activity and are an oblique way of bearing witness to the Master. To serve the younger Churches, too, regardless of any degree of church growth, is commonly accepted as satisfactory mission policy. It occupies the full time of many churchmen.

For all those holding this theory, whether the churches grow or not is of secondary importance. "We are serving Christ" they say. "We are doing kindly acts. We are unselfishly relieving human suffering and rolling back the black curtain of ignorance and illiteracy." Some of this school of thought hold that whether church growth happens or not is none of their business; others that service is the most certain way ultimately to obtain church growth.

A second theory of missions, held in deference to those non-Christians who stridently object to conversion as aggressive arrogance on the part of Christians, says that mission is witness—by word, quiet life, and deed. It is witness to the satisfaction and joy which Christ's redemption has brought. This theory, too, quotes scripture, "Ye are my witnesses," said the Lord. It does not deliberately seek the growth of the Church. It is not aggressive. It does not invite men to become Christians. It simply bears witness to what we know and have experienced. This theory cheerfully invites all nations and all religions to undertake such witness. Let everyone, it says, tell of what God has done for him.

For those holding this view, too, whether the Churches grow or not is a secondary matter. They say, "We bear witness to the saving act of God, whether men hear or whether they do not. None can accuse us of proselytization. God holds us responsible for witness, and it is equally pleasing to Him if we witness where men obey or where they do not."

A third theory is generated by the great causes of today. The battle for brotherhood claims the attention of many Christians. The cause of church union is dear to many hearts. Creating world friendship, ushering in world peace, uniting the rich diversities of the nations into one harmonious whole, and developing world courts and world governments, are dreams which have captured the minds of many disciples of Christ. Extending social justice, so that all men share equally as sons of God, and liberating oppressed masses so that all may have the good things of life, enlist the ardent support of many. Each of these and other similar causes manifests itself in the world mission and develops its own theory of mission.

For such Christians, church union, the extension of brotherhood, and the establishment of peace tend to become the *raison d'être* of missions. According to this third theory the degree of church reproduction obtained is of little importance, provided that, through the efforts of the Christian Churches and their world mission, these great causes are advanced.

A fourth theory rejoices that modern missions have purged old religions of their grosser elements, given them a social conscience, and brought them into a world fellowship. "What matter if we have no growing Church in land X," it says, "our schools and colleges have educated the leadership of that land, our churchmen have given them fellowship, they have imbibed splendid Christian idealism and turned from the crude medieval forms of their religions. Their religious leaders are now men of good will, sensitive to the needs of men, glad for inter-faith comradeship, and pressing on with us to a new high goal for humanity. We rejoice in all such Christianization of cultures." This theory of missions is cool to church growth, and indeed to conversion at all.

The fifth, the "promotional" theory, considers anything "good missions" which brings in money from the Churches. Since the vast enterprise, depending on continuous free will offerings, presents the amazing spectacle of hundreds of millions annually being spent decade after decade for ends which have nothing to do with selfish gain for the donor, his Church, or his nation, we mention this theory with respect. We merely point out that it is neutral toward church growth. Its criterion is not what makes the Churches grow, but what brings the money in.

Historically, the sixth theory of missions has had the widest following. Its chief end has been the salvation of souls, the winning of men and nations to Christ, and the establishment of churches. To share the inestimable benefits of becoming disciples of Christ has been its central driving intention. That Christ become the Redeemer of all, national cultures be purified and enriched by nation-wide allegiance to Him, and indigenous churches be multiplied—these have been the dominating ends of this widespread theory. It creates a climate highly favourable to the reproduction of churches. Indeed, it has been this theory of mission which is responsible for the Church everywhere. It guided Paul, Augustine, Patrick, Judson, Livingstone, and thousands of others.

These six theories are influencing missions today. They may be put into three categories.

(1) *The Pauline philosophy*

This holds that the central continuing purpose of the world mission is winning men and women, tribes and nations, to Jesus Christ and multiplying churches. There are no other chief ends of mission, though men may be healed and kindly deeds done as in the case of the cripple of Lystra. These, however, never form the purpose of mission. Missionaries are not sent out to do these deeds. It is not the business of the church in Antioch to do charity in Corinth, but rather to establish churches there which will overflow with Christian neighbourliness and abound in all the loving service and good works mentioned by Christ in His account of the last judgement. This is the view of the New Testament Church.

(2) *The "Parallel" philosophy*

This says that the world mission consists in great parallel thrusts—of service in the name of Christ, witness to Christ, prosecution of great causes, enlightenment of other religions and cultures, contributions of life and money, and evangelization; that the world mission is as broad as the physical, mental, social, and spiritual needs of man and includes his economic, industrial and political life. Therefore the world mission is equally concerned with any meeting of human need anywhere. A mission to teach men how to double their rice crop has equal weightage with a second to teach them to read and a third to lead them to Christ. A section of the mission which devotes itself to increasing friendship between Hindus and Muslims has equal value with one which brings about union of Thai Churches, and with another which plants 100 new congregations in Formosa. That which might possibly prepare for church growth 100 years from now has equal priority with one now baptizing hundreds of converts and establishing them in scores of congregations.

(3) *The Temporal-Eternal philosophy*

This holds that while the acceptance of the Evangel by the whole world is, indeed, the long range chief goal, in the shifting scene which faces us, other ends must sometimes share the stage as equals with church multiplication. The mighty Church of hundreds of millions, which has been created by God and which did not exist in Paul's day, dare not close its eyes to human need.

This philosophy attempts to relate service to preaching the Gospel and founding the Church, in the same way that Jesus did. He healed the sick because it was not in His nature to ignore them. He could not proclaim the Good News of God and be indifferent to even the temporal needs of God's children. Yet He clearly regarded His mighty works as signs of His Messiahship. He recognized the temporal as temporal and the eternal as eternal. "Great multitudes gathered to hear and to be healed of their infirmities. But He withdrew to the wilderness and prayed." (Luke 5: 15.) After a brief earthly ministry, He set His face resolutely toward Jerusalem and the Cross. This keen sense of priorities and proportion marks His ministry. He was in the world but not of the world. To make service or any other highly commendable labour an end in itself, to assign it disproportionate emphasis, or to allow it to crowd out active persuasion and actual discipling is to depart from Christ's example and to disobey His command.

"Christians," says this philosophy, "are simultaneously working toward the evangelization of the world and living a Christian life in a needy world. Any rigid subordination of all other ends to that of winning the world for Christ might miss opportunities to respond to the temporal world about us as Christians should. Similarly any rigid commitment to 'parallel thrusts' might miss opportunities to lead ready men and nations into eternal life. With the tremendous resources of the Church today, it should be possible to do both all the discipling that can be done and all the good deeds the world needs. However, when resources prove insufficient and the choice has to be made, the eternal has a clear priority with us as it had with our Lord."

These three arrangements (the Pauline, the Parallel, and the

Temporal-Eternal) comprise the three most common philosophies of mission. Each deals in a different way with the unavoidable question of priorities. Each has its protagonists. These philosophies underlie all church and mission action. The continuous intricate process by which the Churches enlist and train men, engage them in world mission, and keep them at work, involves numberless decisions on the basis of one philosophy or the other. Every finance meeting of the Churches and Missions settles specific problems in one direction or the other. These philosophies guide the thinking of all churchmen. They stand at the elbows of church executives and board secretaries and through them exert continuous pressure on the entire expansion of Christianity. Let us look at three examples of their wide influences.

A. They control decisions of the leaders of the younger Churches. These men face the crucial issue of choosing the correct philosophy of missions. They cannot dismiss the choice as one which affects missions and older Churches but not them. The older Churches today send younger Churches large grants of men and money to use as they think best. In addition, younger Churches raise precious resources of their own. The expenditure of all this life is controlled by the philosophy of missions held, the complex judgement as to values, ends, means, and priorities which determine the main directions of action. For example, Churches in the Philippines and other Asian countries are now sending missionaries of their own to other lands. Where are these to go and what are they to do? Will they go to where churches are multiplying or to unripe fields? Will they duplicate the nineteenth and twentieth century patterns of Europe and America? Will they provide their missionaries with jeeps? And their younger Churches with hospitals and colleges? Asian churchmen's judgement as to *what mission really is* will determine the answers to these questions.

B. They determine all remedial action to be taken, based on judgement as to what is wrong. What are the major errors of missions today? Some would answer: failing to develop national leadership, dressing nationals in western clothes, eradicating traditional expressions of joy from their cultures, competition between Churches, too exclusive concern with evangelism and not enough with effecting revolutionary improvement in society, hanging on to control too long, and failing to achieve church union. Men of another camp would say: those are minor errors compared with failing to establish growing churches, carrying on mission work where few become Christian while turning a deaf ear to the pleas of thousands for baptism, teachers, and churches, and being preoccupied with secondary ends while discipling the nations goes unachieved. Which camp is correct? The answer to that key question depends entirely on the philosophy of missions held.

C. They determine the ends to which research is directed. A certain seminary intends to stress research in missions. It wants a man to head the department who "would not be tied by ancient shibboleths but would blaze new trails according to the demands and opportunities of this revolutionary modern world." The seminary's philosphy of missions will determine what the research will be and what kind of a man will do it. Does it hold that the essential task is winning men to the Evangel, witnessing to one's faith, doing good works, promoting church union, or transferring authority to nationals? Is it trying to discover what can be substituted for the spread of the Church? Is "There is no other Name" an ancient shibboleth to be discarded in favour of "All roads lead to God"?

In regard to these fundamental philosophies of mission how are churchmen distributed? By and large, while the "Pauline" view has the support of most churchmen as the ultimate goal and the "Temporal-Eternal" is defended as what they are trying to do now, the "Parallel" is what they actually practise. This summary must be qualified. Some few Churches and Missions do to a large extent practise the "Pauline" philosophy. This is particularly true of a few fairly recent missions and of the largest younger Churches and their assisting missions where the proportion of foreign aid to local resources is small. However, by and large, the "Parallel" is practised.

The extent to which this is true will surprise many. They think they are guided by the "Temporal-Eternal" or "Pauline" philosophy and quickly point to a basic statement of policy which officially aligns them behind it. They are then surprised to find how squarely their budget—the actual distribution of their resources—puts them into the "Parallel" category. Their theory is one thing: their practice is another. The "Parallel" is so persuasive, so easy to fall into, so promotionally profitable that it is what actually gets into operation. Today it distributes most men, money, time, and prayer. It affects the relation of older and younger Churches, it influences the training of the clergy and missionaries, it dictates emphases in Christian education, it controls today, and influences tomorrow.

Let us, then, examine this second point of view on which the world mission is operating more and more. Its essence, which differentiates it from both one and three, is its parallelism. "The six great theories of mission" it would say, "have arisen because they were all needed by man. Who can say which should have priority? The world Church must recognize no priorities. According to time and need, one theory may be stressed more than another, but none has innate priority. All are of equal importance. The success of the venture cannot be measured by the achievements of any one, even such an important one as the growth of the church."

Once "Parallelism" has been accepted, mission is then defined to fit. Thus one great missionary society declares: "The Church exists for one purpose, to be obedient to its Lord, to carry out His work in the world. The Church is the instrument of the global thrust of God. The world wide mission is the whole reason for the existence of the Church." This powerful statement makes mission "the Church doing God's work in the world." Since all good works are God's works, all good works around the world are equally mission. Thus mission in the New Testament sense becomes one of many good labours. "Parallelism" flourishes and church growth languishes.

Let us examine the word "parallel." We wonder if many will really back it. When men use it, do they mean that each one of these ends is actually *equally* important? Or have they been trapped by the "both and" formula so that, friendly to all good things, they find themselves defending "great parallel thrusts?" Do they not merely mean that there are many important things to be done and they would rather not get involved in deciding priorities!

We also wonder whether they realize that "Parallelism" is the antithesis of mission as described in the New Testament. There we see preoccupation with the establishment of churches of believers and a confidence that as these were established all other things needful to man would be supplied, not by the missionary nor by the older Church, but by God. "Seek ye first the Kingdom of God and all these things will be added unto you." Paul is emphatic that if men will but turn to Christ, put to death the flesh, seek the things that are above, and be filled with the Holy Spirit, God's rule among men will arrive and God will supply their need above anything that they can ask or think. This is a very different atmosphere from that of parallel missions.

Thorough going "Parallelism" results in Church establishment becoming merely one among many good tasks. The religion to which men of goodwill belong becomes a matter of secondary importance. If faced with the choice, vividly real in many lands today, of leading thousands into the Church or continuing many good works which effect no church reproduction—"Parallelism" serenely continues "many good works," and leaves the thousands without Christ.

There is an inescapable theological bearing to the matter. The Church and its mission are not man's creation. They are rooted in God. Christians are not free to choose what end they please or what philosophy of mission they will follow. The missionary imperative rests back in the nature of God Himself—Who is concerned with the salvation of sinners, to the ends of the world and at the cost of His Son. Remembering this, can the main continuing aim of mission be other than the discipling of all the peoples of earth? What could be the alternative?

Neither the philosophy nor the theology of "Parallelism" will, we fear, stand investigation. Why, then, is it so widely practised—and believed?

There are many reasons, but a chief one is that the specialized activities of modern missions, good in themselves, excellent as auxiliaries, can readily appear to be sufficient ends and to be justified for themselves alone. They thus lead churchmen astray. Departments of each mission are usually devoted to separate aspects of the Christian task such as evangelism, medicine, agricultural production, education and the like. Sometimes whole missions are devoted to some one of these. Thousands of missionaries are trained as specialists. These departmentalisms can betray the Church into "Parallelism," and sometimes do. It is natural that men defend what they are engaged in. Are these activities, then, a mistake? Let us be clear at this crucial point. The establishment of an organization solely to help the hungry grow more food in a given district may be good. What is bad is the leap of theory arising out of this separate organization which affirms that growing more food for this population is in itself as important and necessary as its discipling. From right activities men leap to wrong theories.

In short, the multifarious good activities of modern missions help lead many churchmen into "Parallelism." They like its broadness but have not faced its weakness. They do not really believe it. They will not, we are confident, defend it. They may, indeed, claim that no one believes it! But they do widely practise it.

Some conservative churchmen like to believe that the theology held by liberal Churches leads them into "Parallelism." There may be some ground for this. But after looking at the evidence we do not find that, on the whole, the more conservative Churches and their missions practise more "Pauline" or "Temporal-Eternal" missions. They, too, are caught in the web. They become just as much committed to "broad parallel thrusts" as the more liberal Churches.

If the church is to grow faster, individual churchmen, church boards, missionary societies, local churches, and assemblies must consciously align their practice with the "Pauline" pattern of missionary action. Any mission board or younger Church that does this, will take a step towards extending the Kingdom of God. Choosing this basic philosophy will not in itself effect great church growth—there are too many other factors concerned. But if the dominant purpose is the discipling of men and women, then the other factors which make for church growth can be discovered, welcomed, and put into operation. Conversely, denominations and churchmen who resolve to have nothing to do with "any such narrow interpretation of the world mission," will neither welcome factors leading to church growth nor put them into action. They will play a small part in the mighty increase of churches which we believe God has in store for the years ahead. They will find themselves a smaller and smaller proportion of the Church.

XI

UNDERSTANDING CHURCH GROWTH

A churchman from India assumes that non-Christian children cannot become Christians without their parents, till he finds that in Congo churches frequently refuse the parents but accept the children as Christians. The few Evangelical Christians in Mexico look with amazement at a million-and-a-half Filipinos who broke with Rome to form the Independent Church of the Philippines. Protestants in Argentina can scarcely believe in the meteoric rise of the entirely indigenous *Iglesia Ni Christo* (Church of Christ) in the Philippines, with its membership of several hundred thousands, its striking church buildings in the cities, and its vigorous Bible-centred evangelism. The Anglican clergy of Uganda, with their huge new Church of hundreds of thousands, comprising half the population of the land and discipled in the last fifty years, can with difficulty comprehend a mission where more missionaries than they have for their whole Church are assigned to a "younger Church" of 1,000 communicants, most of whom are employed with foreign funds and represent scattered conversions over eighty years!

The process by which the Church expands is infinitely varied and complex. There is one major pattern in individualistic western countries, another in people-conscious societies, and still another in Latin America and the Philippines. There probably will be a fourth major pattern when the countries now lying back of the iron and bamboo curtains are again in communication with the world.

The major patterns, moreover, divide and sub-divide, again and again. There is certainly not one American pattern, but many: and not one African pattern but scores. Each denomination has its own way—some more and some less successful—of multiplying churches. In addition, each churchman has his own way. It is well that this should be so, for each population presents a separate situation and each band of Christians goes about the task in a way most suited to it. Hundreds of patterns of church growth arise. To classify them under a few major heads is possible but may do the cause a disservice unless churchmen realize that it is quite as important to know the sub-varieties as the major patterns.

What bearing does this complexity have upon the Gospel? A professor once told his classes, "The missionary need know nothing but the Gospel. There are not many Gospels: there is only one. It is so simple that a child can understand it. The task of the missionary and the Christian in the younger Churches is simply to proclaim it. Faith comes by hearing it. God will add to the Church those who believe." What shall we say to this reasonable and biblical position?

The Gospel is indeed simple. There is one Saviour, Jesus Christ, the Lord. He is the same yesterday, today, and forever. Salvation comes by believing in Him. Nevertheless His Church increases in many different patterns. The church in Antioch grew in a different way from the churches in Jerusalem. Those in Corinth and Ephesus increased in still different ways. Each development had many common strands, but also many unique ones. This is even more true today as the churches penetrate societies whose spread in language, culture, education, income, and degree of Christianization is greater than ever before.

Of this complex process of church growth there is a pitiful paucity of information. The assumption underlying work around the world has been that as churchmen carry on good missions, churches will naturally be established and grow. Good missions have frequently been described. The different patterns of church growth have not. There is much information as to how special tasks of missions are to be carried out—how adults can be made literate, pastors prepared, the level of health raised, the Good News preached, and constitutions controlling the organizational life of the younger Churches written. But of the central task—how the churches reproduce, what makes them grow and stop growing, how this can be measured, and how mission resources may be used for this end—on these vital points little information is available.

Uganda has seen church growth of great magnitude. In less than seventy years most of the population of the central sections of the country has been Christianized. In missionary libraries are accounts of the doings of the missionaries and the religious, cultural, and historical backgrounds in Uganda. Anthropological treatises tell of the tribes. But very little describes step by step how this great Church came into being, in what responsiveness consisted, how the movement spread, how churches were organized, how the ministry was trained and self-support developed. Uganda is typical of many younger Churches.

Paucity of information on church growth is due in part to the fact that churchmen know only their own system. Patterns of church growth are the result of the labours of many men. They do not change easily. Churchmen working in one area get to know their own pattern and often feel that it is the only good pattern, or at least the only one with which they are concerned. They are limited by it. If it produces 50 per cent church growth, that is good; and if it produces 10 per cent church growth that also is good. That is "just the way things are here." Two younger Churches, separated by fifty miles only, and working amongst the same kind of people, often show very different rates of growth. In the same decade one will demonstrate an increase of 250 per cent and the other an increase of 19 per cent. It will never occur to the 19 per-center to shift to the pattern which is currently bringing in 250 per cent a decade fifty miles away. "They have their way of going about things, and we have ours" is more likely to be said.

The lack of information is due in part to the fact that those who are most successful in making the Church grow are so burdened with the "care of the churches" that they have no time to write. Paul seldom finds his Luke. The "thin red line" of churchmen becomes thinnest where the greatest ingatherings are going on. It is also due to the difference of pattern. "That may work over there," is frequently said, "but our circumstances are different." There is a measure of truth in the statement. Situations are indeed different and they change from decade to decade. What is written about the pattern by which Church A is growing will be fully applicable only in Population A. So the incentive to write for others is low. To some extent each set of churchmen must work out its own pattern. When to this is added the difficulty and cost of publication in younger Church fields where every dollar is scrutinized, it seems inevitable that little should be published on how the churches grow.

But much could be published. Allowing for a degree of difference in each population, all churchmen will benefit by being informed how the churches are actually increasing in other areas. Pattern A may not be fully applicable in Population N, but it will be pertinent at many points. Churchmen could render no greater service to the younger Churches than to describe and publish significant data in cases of church growth. Such Christian literature will have immediate and far-reaching effect on the increase of the churches.

The need for English, German and Swedish materials of this sort is great enough; but information in the vernaculars is even more necessary. Average leaders of the younger Churches speak little English. They speak their own languages. Even more than English speaking men, they know exclusively their own pattern. If that produces church growth, good; if it does not, that also is good. They get no information about how other Churches are multiplying. They imagine theirs the only possible pattern of increase. Frequently the denominational pattern inherited from their western mother Church—whether it produces growth in their particular conditions or not—is better known to them than successful indigenous patterns a few miles away. Vernacular publications of church growth studies would help greatly in breaking down this insularity.

Theological seminaries usually teach church history, holding that it is important for ministers to know how the Churches came into being. Curiously, such presentations of the ways in which the Churches grew, the doctrines which they cherished, and the organizational form which they found most congenial, are generally limited to ancient Churches—in other lands. The acts studied are those of churchmen many years ago among shadowy and unreal peoples. Yet the information of supreme value to the Church in Nyasaland, let us say, is how Nyasaland churches are being created and what patterns God has blessed there during these last fifty years. How people turned to Christ 100 years ago is not so important. How they turned 1,500 years ago is even less so. But how they are turning now, during these galloping decades, how congregations are now being established, and how Christian education now turns out multipliers of the Church—all this is vitally important. Little such church history is being taught. Little indeed is known about it.

People-movements are by no means the only method of church growth; but they are the pattern by which well over two-thirds of the younger Church all around the world has arisen. Yet so great is the dearth of information as to how churches actually multiply that *The Bridges of God*[1], describing people-movements and defending them as one valid way of increasing the Church, came to many churchmen as a revelation—and appeared to some as a provocative, debatable book!

The pattern of church growth common to the Assemblies of God has been used of God in several Latin American countries mightily to increase the Church. Yet few leaders of other Churches can accurately describe that pattern. Some seem satisfied with describing it as "pentecostal" and supposing that its virtue lies solely in the ejaculatory aspects of its worship! The point is even more significant if, in Latin America, to the successful congregations of the Assemblies of God be added the vigorously growing congregations of the Southern Baptists, Methodists, Disciples, and others. What makes these Latin American churches grow with power? How do they instruct their members so that these go out to reach others? How do they create a ministry which is self-supporting? How do they use resources from abroad so that the indigenous Church is energized, not debilitated? The answer to these questions about these particular churches are surely of the essence of the training of churchmen for work in Latin America; but we doubt if they are available in any theological seminary or missionary training institution.[2]

At the great theological conference at Bangkok in 1956, which brought together seminarians from many countries of South-East Asia, many subjects were discussed. Evangelism received minor mention, largely in theological and theoretical terms. One longed

---

[1] *The Bridges of God*, by D. A. McGavran, 7s. 6d., World Dominion Press.

[2] Those excellent books, *The Indigenous Church in Peru*, by John Ritchie (World Dominion Press), *The Indigenous Church*, by M. L. Hodges (The Gospel Publishing House, Springfield, Mo., USA), and *Missionary Methods*, by Roland Allen (World Dominion Press), should be studied by churchmen in Latin America and elsewhere. They describe one of the successful patterns of missions.

to hear of proved cases of church growth, what was bringing them about, and how the problems which growth throws at the Church were being solved. In one country represented, several vigorous movements to Christ, by both individual and group conversion, were flourishing. They constituted the very quintessence of all churchmanship—the Church mightily reproducing and turning people of the world into the Household of God. Yet there was only the briefest mention of these movements and no discussion at all as to how ministers in training in South-East Asia could profit by study of these gracious acts of God.

What part does training play in producing men who make the churches multiply?

To date it has played chiefly a negative part. Great denominations —East and West—secure in hundreds of thousands of members, and burdened with the care of their existing churches, train their clergymen chiefly in how to shepherd the existing flocks. It can be taken as a truism that missionaries and nationals come out of seminaries heavily biased toward perfecting what has been gathered. Even those whom God lays hold of as apostles to the Gentiles are likely to leave Gamaliel's feet knowing more about how the people of God may be led farther along the pilgrim way than about how people of the world may be led to Christ.

The World Church today carries this process a step further. Large numbers of missionaries are given from one to five years' training for some special task judged helpful to a given mission or younger Church. Hundreds of specialists in agriculture, medicine, education and production are annually sent abroad on missions of philanthropy and inter-church aid, but they are quite untrained in bringing any person to Christian faith and obedience.

The courses and disciplines of many seminaries are not producing and cannot produce the kind of churchmen who will tackle the total evangelization of the world. Graduates may be competent in social engineering, ecumenicity, pastoral care of western flocks, Greek exegesis and worship in a beautifully appointed church with two choirs; but they are likely to know little about the way in which the younger Churches to which they go have arisen and are arising, and the processes which in them are victoriously winning individuals and groups to Christian discipleship. They are likely to have little enthusiasm for total evangelization and church extension and much for some aspect of the world mission being stressed when they received their theological training. Church union, transfer of authority to nationals, the application of "religion" to all of life, and the rise of the younger Churches, have become common slogans in institutions for the training of churchmen for the world mission; at the same time "the evangelization of the world in this generation" has disappeared from their classrooms and chapels. No thinking of a similar magnitude has taken its place. The exciting challenge of making disciples of all nations has evaporated. Students are not studying the ripened fields of earth. They are not being taught to discern and harvest these. What they are taught makes them indifferent toward the total evangelization of nations. They regard it as irrelevant.

This is tragedy for any Church. It is double tragedy for the younger Churches. Since so many of them constitute a very small part of the total population of their countries, their major business is to grow. Theological education which does not make its graduates competent in church multiplication today emasculates the ministry. In the days that lie ahead, should any segment of the population of Land A become responsive, it will probably be approached by the local Churches. If among the seminarians in Land A, training has atrophied the passion to multiply churches, the world Church is likely to stand on the outside, either not hearing of the opportunity or helpless to do anything about it.

Much is said today about the ecumenical spirit and church union. One great advantage of the ecumenical spirit is that it bridges the chasms of exclusiveness which surround the various Branches of the Church. Church union should do this even more effectively. Once done, the inhibitions which prevent one Branch from putting into practice successful patterns of church growth originating in another Branch should disappear. The truly ecumenical Church will claim as its own any good pattern of any other Church. "For all are Christ's and Christ is God's." Among ecumenically minded Churches, information about church growth and development therefore is—theoretically at any rate—freed from denominational prejudices. If any method proves successful in the discipling of the peoples, ecumenical Churches should not scorn it because it is used by a sister Church even if that sister Church is not friendly toward the present ecumenical movement.

The extension of the Kingdom of God, then, demands the accurate description of all patterns of church increase. Wide sharing of this vital information by conferences, lectures, courses in seminaries, publication of case studies of growing Churches, and every other way is essential. The understanding by every churchman of how God is causing churches to multiply is a *sine qua non* for church growth.

The extension of the Kingdom of God demands research into church growth. As Professor Latourette has well said:

> Surely no other enterprise demands for its larger usefulness, more continuous, fearless, honest and painstaking investigation of the conditions which it confronts and of its methods and results. To these investigations should be brought all the best and latest techniques with which scholarship and the scientific approach have provided us.

An enterprise which spends hundreds of millions a year should spend hundreds of thousands each year in research as to how it is getting on *with its central task*. The results of such research will repay a hundredfold all that can be put into it. The Church can afford to do no less.

XII

THE "CULTURAL OVERHANG"

Had this chapter been written in Latin America it would have been called the Shadow of the North, or in Pakistan, the Shadow of the West. Now that the younger Churches are sending missionaries, however, the shadow cannot be described as coming from any one direction. So we speak of the "cultural overhang" of the land from which missionaries go forth. It has a profound effect on church growth.

A group of students crowded the Yale Divinity School hall plying the missionary with questions about South America. "You were describing, sir, the fervent nature of much Latin American Protestantism. I could not tell whether you approved of this or not. To us it seems a rather undesirable feature. Is there not a danger that sentimentality becomes a substitute for the prophetic Christianity needed to revolutionize life and lift it to a Christian level?" These students were exhibiting "cultural overhang." American training had formed in them a high opinion of a prophetic Christianity which revolutionized society. Their heroes were men who practised this kind of Faith. They were confident that this was good for the United States and would be good for Latin America. The enemy of such prophetic Christianity was, they thought, emotional Christianity. This they believed was true in North America. They presumed it was true in Latin America. This is "cultural overhang." To a degree often unsuspected, churchmen assume that what they know as good for their own church or society is universally good.

A missionary grew up in a modern church school in Iowa; and was then assigned to a younger Church which had bogged down to a 30 per cent increase in a land where other churches were obtaining great growth. He was shocked to find that his churches used uniform Sunday School lessons. The young people's work also was "much too serious" according to American standards. He concluded that his major task was lifting the standard of religious education. He assumed that, as this was done, great church growth would follow naturally as it did in the churches he knew in America. He threw himself into his task and did excellent work. But he failed to observe: (*a*) that in Iowa fine religious education increases church membership from children of the Protestant community; and (*b*) that in the younger Churches round about him rapid growth resulted when the members continuously sought people of the world and brought them into the fellowship of Christians. Thus as he focused the attention of his churches on educational procedures, he crowded out the very activities which in his adopted land were essential to winning from the world. Instead of lifting his churches to the 100 per cent a decade growth the other Evangelical Churches were achieving, he diminished the rate of growth from thirty to ten. "Cultural overhang" had led, unintentionally and unnecessarily, in the wrong direction.

In the United States, new churches are constantly being planted. Varieties of evangelistic campaigns are continually in operation, gaining new members, organizing new congregations, and erecting new buildings. This evangelism is devised for, and successful in, a population which is already nominally Christian, holds the Bible to be "the Scriptures," and the Church to be desirable. It is a kind of evangelism suited to American society. "Cultural overhang" assumes that this kind of evangelism will lead men to Christ everywhere. The facts are otherwise.

A discerning Filipino said, "Western evangelism is little more than well organized gathering in of existing friends; but the kind of evangelism we need must convince Roman Catholics, both active and nominal, that the Evangelical Church is the Church of Jesus Christ, His apostles, and the New Testament." To be effective among animists, evangelism must convince them—often by considerations which would have no effect in the West—that the Christian faith is the pearl of great price. The evangelism which wins hard-core Marxists for Christ is very different from that which "in the territory comity assigns us" organizes a church in Middletown, Texas.

Churchmen trained in America get an American understanding of evangelism and conversion. This has only limited value in other lands. It may, indeed, hinder church growth there. While the Evangel is the same for all nations, it must be divested of the "cultural overhang" of other lands and presented in garments which clarify its message and bring men to commitment. Paul clearly recognizes "cultural overhang" when he writes:

> I have made myself a slave to all, that I might win the more. To the Jews I became as a Jew. . . . To those outside the law I became as one outside the law. To the weak I became weak, that I might win the weak. I have become all things to all men, that I might by all means save some.

A doctor of philosophy from the West, on reaching his field, was assigned to train men with six to eight years of schooling to become pastors of village churches and preachers to rural non-Christians. His professors in America had been convinced that Christianity must make its adjustment to the scientific age by explaining the miraculous in the Scriptures in terms agreeable to the scientific mind. The doctor passed on this point of view to his preachers in training, despite the fact that both they and the non-Christians they met were not in the least troubled by the miraculous element in the Scriptures. Indeed, the non-Christians believed fully in their own scriptures, where even fourth-rate gods performed exuberant miracles besides which those of the New Testament seemed tame. His students' effectiveness among that population was greatly diminished. The doctor was a victim of "cultural overhang." So were his students and the churches they later served.

Liberalism is a product of a certain type of western society in a certain stage. It intends to train scientific minded men to meet the needs of scientific minded society. When such men go to the lands of the younger Churches, they often find themselves at work among people who have, instead of the scientific viewpoint, a medieval or sometimes a premedieval mind. Theology fashioned and fitted to highly advanced sections of a scientific west does not touch the well-springs of action among such a population. It takes something much more biblical and direct to induce movement.

"Ah but," exclaims someone, "are you not forgetting the great advance in science which the East is making, the hundreds of thousands of university graduates, and the tens of thousands who return each year from the top colleges of the West. We must have a Christian theology which commends itself to these sons of the twentieth century." This is again the voice of the "cultural overhang." But do nationals and missionaries who preach "a Gospel adapted to scientific minded men" win more of the scientific minded easterners than others who preach a more biblical faith?

We are not here aligning ourselves with liberalism or fundamentalism. We are underlining the fact that what looks right and true to some in the milieu of high scientific achievement looks irrelevant or maybe even wrong to men in pre-scientific cultures.

Some western churchmen today regard the numerical growth of the churches as a matter of indifference. What counts is Christian action and Christian character. If any church has these, numerical increase will take care of itself.

For the time being, let us grant that for the West—or any land where Christians comprise a large part of the population—this affirmation is true and should form a working basis for the Church; but this does not mean it is universally true. In the East—or in any land where one in a hundred is a Christian—the chief purpose of the younger Church should be (as Paul's was) to persuade men, through word and deed, that Jesus is the Christ. Accessions should be a chief and unavoidable criterion of success. In such a situation, trying to change the structure of non-Christian society, decrying the significance of numerical increase, and spending large resources for inconsiderable church growth is to dwarf and retard the younger Church. If this "cultural overhang" is not discerned and discarded, churches will not multiply.

In the United States today, the movement to look upon Protestants, Catholics, and Jews as one big family of God has captured certain groups of Protestants. The latter in an effort to wipe out un-Christian prejudice against Roman Catholics and Jews, assume that all three have equally good "religions." This attitude affects Protestants in Latin America, first the missionaries and then the nationals, and the increase of the churches is delayed.

In this connection, the tremendous increase of the Assemblies of God can, in part, be explained. They believe that the gift of the Holy Spirit is necessary to full Christian life, and that theirs is the only Church which makes it available: they are quite sure that nominal Christians in North as well as South America need converting. Hence in Latin America they have no hesitation in working for the conversion of Roman Catholics. Their cultural overhang is favourable to the growth of churches in Latin America.

The 1897 report of the British and Foreign Bible Society writes of the Church in Korea:

> Probably most of the candidates for baptism have anything but commendable motives for joining the church. That may be freely conceded. Yet one rejoices in their numbers. Their sense of sore need, whether spiritual or earthly, drives them in, and they are therefore more or less teachable.

The thousands who were thus gathered in were purified in the fires of the great revival which swept Korea six to ten years later. American standards, we think, caused the missionaries to judge that "the motives of the candidates were anything but commendable"; but fortunately, the missionaries overcame this overhang, baptized the converts, and set about perfecting them. Had the church leaders in 1896 succumbed to their overhang and rejected the converts, the 1905–1910 opportunity for church growth so well described by Methodist Wasson in *Church Growth in Korea* and by Presbyterian Goforth in *When the Spirit's Fire Fell on Korea*, would probably have come and gone without yielding any multiplication of churches.

Many church leaders in America, looking at themselves and the current scene, are deeply impressed with the ineffectiveness of multitudes of Christians. These seem impotent to avert war, stop juvenile delinquency, bring about economic justice, or usher in full inter-racial brotherhood. Pondering this weakness of confessed Christians, leaders develop and put forward as of primary importance a whole complex of doctrines, attitudes, slogans, and priorities calculated to explore the meaning of Christianity for all of life, search out for modern man the solutions Christianity offers, and apply them fearlessly. These are sound enough—for America where a large majority of the people are at least nominally Christian and enjoy considerable achievements in production, education, and communications.

Similarly many church leaders in Europe, believing that, at least to some extent, they live in "post-Christian Europe," and facing the judgement of multitudes that the Church is irrelevant, develop and put forward as of primary importance another whole complex of doctrines, attitudes, slogans and priorities. These are sound enough—for Europe. Because Europe and America are alike in many respects, each complex overlaps the other.

Victims of "cultural overhang"—and their name is legion—judge that these complexes conceived in specific situations suit all lands. The priorities worked out for lands where huge Churches are secure are applied to lands where tiny Churches live in constant danger. The fashion in Christian thinking which fits the western scene becomes the intellectual equipment which missionary candidates and visiting nationals obtain in western seminaries.

In short, the situation in which each church generation finds itself greatly influences its doctrines, emphases and enthusiasms. These become its common Christian assumptions. They do further the growth and welfare of the Churches in the specific populations, times, and places where they have arisen; but they are not nearly as beneficial elsewhere. In other times and places, they may even damage the growth and welfare of the Churches.

The churchman, coming new to his field from the West, is specially likely to err because of overhang. He is often appalled at the lack of achievement of the churches to whose service he is assigned. He measures these against the idealism of his seminary. He has no equipment for measuring them against their former condition. He is often offended by the sub-Christian behaviour of new converts. It is usually easier to see the faults of predecessors than their virtues and consequently there is purging of the rolls, getting down to what we really have, stopping this ill-considered influx of baptized pagans, lifting the standards, making Christianity mean something, and all the rest. Such culture-caused reactions are seldom helpful. They shift the delicate balance which is bringing in new disciples and count stoppage of growth as a positive gain, when actually it is a defeat of the first magnitude.

Let churchmen recognize "cultural overhang." He who is conscious of it need not succumb to it. Let him separate it from himself, hang it up in the sunlight, examine it from the point of view of the growth and welfare of the younger Church concerned and determine its usefulness or otherwise.

Let churchmen adopt a pragmatic attitude toward methods. Those methods which work are good. The "best" methods which do not profit the Church should be discarded—they are not best.

The most "unlikely" methods which do profit the Church should be embraced—they are the best.[1]

And what is it to "profit the church"? Many aspects of the Church come to mind. Numerical increase is not the only one. There is unquestionably growth in grace, self-support, and education, as well as growth in membership. However, if the criterion of growth in numbers is discarded completely—as it frequently is—and leaders of the younger Churches propose to determine what is profitable to the Church on *wholly* other grounds, they run against a practical difficulty. Activities congenial to their cultural overhang come easily and seem right to them. Hence they are continued. Once the numerical increase of the Church is discarded as one but not the only criterion, almost any helpful activity can be abundantly justified, even if it stops church growth in the midst of great opportunity. Thus we see a Church in Puerto Rico standing for sixteen years at a membership of 4,000. Its ministerial leaders and missionary assistants have been actively at work doing many things which are "good for the Church"; but one suspects these are done more because of cultural overhang than because they are genuinely good for the Church. If they were really good for the Church, could it stand still for sixteen years in the midst of great numbers of winnable people?

"Cultural overhang" is well recognized by missionary writers, but is usually confined to Western customs, likes and dislikes, habits of living, and attitudes toward people. All of these are without question important. We go further, however, and suggest that much thinking profitable to churches in one land may be detrimental to churches in another. The philosophy of the great successful Churches of the scientific West simply does not fit the Churches which have arisen among the masses of pre-scientific people. Neither does it fit the tiny educated leadership of those masses.

Well-fed, middle-aged churchmen from Ohio need to limit the amount they eat lest they grow fat. Following this way of life, they

[1] A pragmatic attitude toward method is advocated here—not toward the bed-rock verities of historic Christianity. These remain true whether they seem to work or not. God was in Christ reconciling the world to Himself both when our Lord was dying on the Cross and the disciples had fled and when 3,000 were baptized on the day of Pentecost. But the methods of mission, so dependent on many factors in the situation and so affected by the culture of the witness, can profitably be weighed against the degree to which they achieve their intended end.

develop convictions about food, habits of eating, and a jargon about calories, waistlines, pounds and diets. This is good for them. But it would be calamitous to apply it to peasant boys in church boarding schools in India. They need all the food they can get and much more fat than it is ever possible to buy. The well-fed middle-aged churches of the West develop all kinds of convictions about God and man, the Church and the world, what Christians should do, and how Churches grow. These are, we trust, good for them. But it would be calamitous to apply these convictions, habits and fashions to young Churches in other lands.

Nationals and missionaries training in the West need particularly to bear this in mind. In estimating what is good for their churches, they must beware of taking at face value the current conclusions of the Churches of the West. They should allow for "cultural overhang."

XIII

THE TREMENDOUS PRESSURE TO "PERFECT"

Two forces constantly press on the Church. One pushes it into shepherding the flock and perfecting its own life, the other into discipling the nations and spending itself for others.

These forces are not evenly balanced. There is a constitutional bias toward perfecting. The Churches gravitate toward caring for what they have. Their built-in nature prefers perfecting. It is easier for the Church to settle down to a quiet shepherding of the flock than to climb uphill to missionary endeavour. This is often true of missionaries themselves. Sent out to win the world for Christ, they settle down with a small, non-growing congregation, convinced that their truest duty lies in lifting its membership to new heights of Christian living.

Let us look at the case for perfecting. Over 90 per cent of the teaching of our Lord deals with perfecting man and society. He addressed Himself to Israel—the people of God—teaching them in every way what their high status involved. The availability of God, His love for men, the inwardness of true religion, the need to serve fellow men, the measureless value of the soul—all these and many other themes pour in profusion from His lips. But there is little exhortation to win others to discipleship and none directly to multiply churches.

In the Epistles we observe even greater emphasis on Christian living. Each letter is addressed to those already Christian. Each deals with how they are to become better Christians. Paul's great theme is: "You are chosen by God, bought with a price, freed from sin, redeemed by Christ, born again saints of God. Be what you are." Few are his calls to missionary endeavour.

The life of the Christian from the beginning has cried aloud for ever greater apprehension of the mind of Christ. Compared with the divine life to which the Christian is called, his actual achievements continually shame him. What wonder that spiritual leaders, like Paul himself, pour themselves out in prayer that God will grant a mighty increase of strength by His Spirit in the inner man "to the saints who are (already) faithful in Jesus Christ."

This urge to perfection is strong enough where the preacher and his flock are the same kind of people, fellow citizens of the same state, at about the same level of cultural development. But where church leaders are highly favoured Christians of an advanced society and are working among less favoured Christians out of a backward one, there they feel the urge to perfect their converts ever more keenly. Many younger Churches are marked by this disparity. Their leaders (whether nationals, trained for many years in mission schools and theological seminaries, or missionaries) are so different from the rank and file of the membership, a large percentage of whom may be illiterate, that the pressure for perfecting as the main task is overwhelming. Notable ingathering becomes difficult even in ripened harvest fields.

Does this mean that discipling is in truth a secondary task? Should Churches concentrate on "the more important task" of teaching all things to those who have been baptized? Certainly across the lands of the younger Churches, except where the Church is growing rapidly, "looking after what we have" comes to be the all-absorbing task. This is what "missions" frequently are satisfied to attempt. Now that churches have been planted in every land of earth, is not the central task that of so perfecting them that they shine with divine lustre and thus draw all men to themselves? Is this not the teaching of the New Testament?

Before we answer these questions let us look at the case for discipling.

Despite the fact that over 90 per cent of the Gospels and Epistles exhort the spiritual development of disciples of Christ, the New Testament as a whole is one long record of outreach. It begins with God's outreach across the gulf which separates humanity from deity. It continues through the sacrificial death of the Lord Jesus who, deliberately turning from teaching the household of God that which was necessary for it to know, "steadfastly set His face" toward the Cross that He might create a new community of the redeemed. The men who came into this community and were filled with His

Spirit, despite the plenitude of His recorded teachings toward perfecting, and despite the paucity of His recorded commands toward discipling, immediately went out to find others and bring them to Christ. When, because of their faith in Christ, they were beaten and their houses were burned, they went to their kinsmen and urged them to accept the wonderful privilege of becoming Christians. Pharisees, confident of their racial superiority, on accepting Christ became special messengers to races they had scorned. They went out to reach the inferior and win the foolish and the weak. They did not exhort others to win men for Christ. But others who had received the Holy Spirit did the same without exhortation. It seems to have been necessary to tell men to crucify the works of the flesh and manifest the fruit of the spirit; but it does not seem to have been necessary to tell them to win others. They did that eagerly. Their life in Christ constrained them to bring men into the fold.

The declared universality of the Gospel also requires the expansion of the Church. The teaching of the Bible is that there is salvation in Christ and in none other. Christ's salvation is for all men. He commanded His followers to make disciples of all peoples. Discipling must be given a very large place in every Church and Mission if this is to occur.

The tug-of-war between perfecting and discipling takes place in a world full of potential church growth. The clash of religious thinking was never greater. The hammer of Communism has fallen heavily on many a cherished defence of many a religion. The Koran sells in Western book-stores and the Bible all over the world. Hindu philosophers lecture in Western universities and Hindu temples rise in American cities. Into the whirlpool of today's religious and philosophical speculation flow currents from many religions. What river will flow out of it? Will it be syncretism? Toynbee thinks so, and he is widely read and believed. Will it be Hinduism? This ancient religion believes it is wide enough for the whole world. Will it be Buddhism (200,000 Hindus embraced Buddhism in 1956)? Or Islam? Many Muslims are astir with the hope that Islam can march again. Or will it be Evangelical Christianity?

Is this the right time to rivet the attention of the churches on bringing their present following to perfection; or does the ripening world call us to press forward with discipling?

In asking this question, we must remember that perfecting may develop into "legalism." We are in danger of "loading on the law" as a requirement of accepting Christ. That is neither good missionary practice nor good theology. The burden of the law—do this and don't do that—is so great that neither we nor our fathers could bear it. Faith in Christ is something different. It is something inherent in becoming disciples. It is not, of course, receiving grace that we should sin more; but it *is* receiving grace, not a legal code.

The pressure to perfect operates on all Churches, older and younger. It induces the older Churches in the West and the East to lavish care on themselves, pressing forward feverishly to better and ever better church buildings, programmes, Christian education and service enterprises. It bears down on the vast missionary programme thrusting it ever more certainly into channels of service to the already established younger Churches. It also bears down on the younger Churches pushing them from three directions into this programme of perfection: (*a*) it exerts a quiet control on fraternal inter-church aid to assure that a suitably large amount is used for existing younger Churches; (*b*) it operates so that a very great part of the giving of the younger Churches themselves goes back into their local church programmes; (*c*) it ensures that most of their missionary giving is spent in their own mission fields for care of those already Christian.

It would be a most interesting exercise to divide up the giving of the world Church to show how much of it went to perfecting existing churches and Christians, to benevolent service of people of the world, to evangelism which made few converts, and to evangelism showing some success in making disciples of the nations. If anyone will analyse the budget of his own Church or Mission Board, he will find abundant evidence of this steady pressure to perfect.

The Church is encouraged to perfect in a day of tremendous opportunity to disciple. Which shall she do?

"She should both perfect and disciple" is both the traditional and the true answer; but it misses the main point. In order to do both, she must deliberately emphasize discipling. It is frightfully easy for any Church—younger perhaps more than older—to slip into heartfelt perfecting and casual discipling—even in the face of tremendous opportunity.

A missionary was stressing to her board the need for discipling. An influential member became quite agitated lest the board embark on a programme entirely dedicated to discipling and neglect the spiritual development of the existing congregations. He need not have feared. The balances *are so weighted* that there is much more danger of the Church neglecting discipling than neglecting its own spiritual development. Churchmen are so sensitive to the need for spiritual development of existing Christians that perfecting runs little danger of being neglected.

An American, returning from a short visit to Africa, said:

> Because Christianity turns out to be less than Africans thought it was, many who would become converts turn away from it. We must therefore make the Church really a fulfilment of the dream of men at their best. Making it more uplifting, more just and brotherly—this is the real battle. As the Church gets better, it will win converts of itself.

Hearts warm to such an exhortation to further perfecting of Christianity, but it is not really where we have failed. It asserts that more Africans would become Christians if Christianity had more to offer. Is this true? During the last 100 years 3,000,000 Yorubas became Muslims. This was most certainly not because Islam offered more than Christianity. Islam did not offer education, medicine, social conscience, emancipation of womanhood, moral power, or freedom from superstition—to say nothing of forgiveness of sins and the gift of the Holy Spirit. Animistic Africans from 10,000 villages did not measure both religions with the yardstick of Christ and then become Muslims. There is no reason to believe that, had some further perfecting of existing Christians in America and Nigeria taken place, these 3,000,000 Yorubas would have automatically poured into the Christian Church. Evidence is all the other way. These Yorubas could have been won for Christ—but when they were winnable the world mission, busy in many other good works elsewhere, was providing one missionary to 50,000 Nigerians, and he, poor fellow, was so busy perfecting hundreds who accepted Christ that he did not have time or strength to take in the thousands who could have been won. Massive ingathering was needed, not an improvement of Christian doctrine or practice.

The heart of the matter is the proportion of effort to be given to perfecting and discipling. All agree both should be done. Disagreement lies in the proportion and timing. We shall make five comments on this aspect of the matter.

Five comments

First, discipling and perfecting are frequently intertwined. When both are going on in the same population it is hard to say where one ends and the other begins. Nevertheless, because of the built-in preference for perfecting, churchmen should be alert to see that discipling does not decay, and does, in fact, continue vigorous.

Second, we must recognize that all discipling involves some perfecting and can be a high form of it. There is no better way to increase conviction, knowledge of the Bible, and Christian character than to win others to Christian faith. He who is persuading others is much more likely to take his faith seriously than he who is concentrating attention on himself. Effort devoted to discipling is addressed to the highest form of spiritual development, not diverted from it.

Let us see this in the concrete. Here is a cluster of congregations of Mandarin-speaking Chinese among responsive fellows. For seven years it has grown at over 100 per cent. The processes of this expansion—cottage prayer meetings, open-air preaching, tract distribution, individual witness, study of the Bible, and other activities—over and above any increase of the *koinonia* they may effect—cause great *spiritual development of the existing Christians.* The cottage-prayer meeting concerned with the salvation of friends from the world is a better instrument of Christian attainment than one concerned exclusively with the interior life of the Christians. Discipling is a high form of perfecting. Resources allocated to discipling are in reality allocated to major increase of Christian quality of life.

Bishop Pickett, for a long time the chairman of the National Christian Council in India, says: "Perfecting the saints is impossible without discipling. People who do not win converts do not prosper spiritually. Wherever I have seen Christians concentrating on perfecting their own life and neglecting their mission, there I have seen people going backward spiritually."

Third, perfecting often hinders discipling. True, it sometimes assists discipling, particularly where church growth is going on; but it is common for churches to get wrapped up in types of perfecting which result in no discipling at all. Where the population is not very responsive and there are relatively abundant mission resources, tremendous expenditures of mission effort in a perfecting which does not break through to discipling is a common phenomenon in the world mission. Loving assistance of congregations which seldom have a conversion from the world, training ministers who are content with or resigned to non-growing churches, and rich services to the people of the world in the vicinity of such churches, absorb disproportionately large shares of the men and money of Mission and Church. When this takes place in the face of open doors and ripening fields, perfecting hinders discipling.

Fourth, during periods of expansion when the Faith is surging forward in some population, if any part of the task must suffer it should be perfecting. At such times discipling has first priority. Perfecting will happen later, if ingathering happens first. Suppose that, following Pentecost, the small band of inexperienced church leaders had said: "No more baptizing now. No more preaching on the streets and in the temple. No arresting miracles. Our task is clear. This great horde of 3,000 new Christians must first understand the teaching of Christ, be organized into well functioning congregations, and given a trained ministry." We look also at Paul. In church after church, where perfecting was barely begun, after a few weeks or months, he would depart to engage in further discipling. When the churches can increase, winning the winnable must, for the time being, take the larger share of the total effort.

Fifth, responsibility for determining proportions falls on Missions and Churches. The Church or Mission Board which spends £100,000 today—or allocates it in a budget session—inescapably makes apportionment of effort. It makes it in a day of tremendous opportunity for church growth and tremendous pressure to perfect. This heightens its responsibility.

The twentieth century has greatly increased the pressure to perfect. A deeper understanding of the mind of Christ, and a surer control of society and nature, have combined to create a new standard of Christian quality, which may not be achieved but is thought to be achievable. This, like fire under a boiler, generates pressure to perfect. When 90 per cent of German Christians neither had, nor could read, Bibles, they would have thought 90 per cent illiteracy among their African Christian brethren quite normal. Now, when 98 per cent of the German Christians are fully literate, they are naturally troubled at 50 per cent illiteracy among African Christians and ask, "Shall we take in more people or teach those we have to read the Bible?" When a Scots minister could pray: "From ghoulies and ghosties and long legged beasties and things that go oomp in the dark, good Lord deliver us," a high degree of belief in evil spirits among the members of the younger Church would have appeared acceptable. But today, to men trained in our science-conscious West, a small degree of such belief raises the question, "Are we justified in calling these baptized pagans Christian and should we not stop all further baptisms and devote ourselves to perfecting?"

We can see this pressure to perfect in many seminaries. They are occupied in making their students dissatisfied with current Christianity. As long as war, racial animosity, economic injustice, and lust exist among church-members, these seminaries deprecate any outreach for new members. We have sympathy with such a passion for righteousness; but must point out that graduates of these institutions with their emphasis on perfection, are biased against the making of new disciples.

The heightened standards of a highly scientific, highly comfortable, and highly perfected church leadership—Eastern and Western—are brought to bear on the younger Churches exactly at a time when multitudes of men all about them are in the valley of decision and are marching out of their old faiths. Again and again, in country after country, conscientious questions like the following burst from modern churchmen facing unprecedented opportunity for church growth and plagued by the pressures to perfect. "Must we not stop now and perfect those already Christian? How can we take in more? With the limited resources sent out by our Church dare we risk expansion?" This is where the problem bites. If church growth is desired, those questions must be answered so that perfecting does not shut out discipling but accompanies it.

Answers may be on several levels. The historical answer would be: nations, where large majorities are now Christian, started on the upward trail with what we would count today a deplorably low degree of Christianization. They could have started nowhere else. That is the meaning of "babes in Christ." So take all who come, just as parents accept all babies which come, as fast as they come, and give them the best nurture possible. Do not stop taking them in because you are dissatisfied with the standard of nurture immediately available. God's arm is not shortened. He will not leave His people ignorant.

The modern answer might be: the new world will certainly lift men out of illiteracy, poverty, sickness, and superstition. Look at the tremendous surge of progress going on in China, Africa, India, and almost every other land. In addition, the world Church through inter-Church aid, fraternal delegates, world conferences, and scores of other forms of stimulation, makes the continued progress of Christians everywhere even more likely than that of non-Christians. So take them in, fearing nothing.

The statistical answer would be: no church population is homogeneous and equally advanced in the things of the spirit. In the most backward groups there are gloriously perfect Christians. It is worth taking in 100,000 to get 5,000 mature Christians, even if the rest remain for some time babes in Christ. So take them in. Wheat comes wrapped in chaff. Winnowing belongs to God.

The competitive answer would be: there are millions on the

march. They are going somewhere, Buddhism, Islam, Communism, Hinduism, Roman Catholicism, or Evangelical Christianity. There is much more chance of their becoming true born-again Christians out of Evangelical Faith than out of any other system, so take them in and, as fast as you can, teach them all things whatsoever He has commanded us.

The theological answer flings back in our face a battery of questions. What saves? Is it disbelief in evil spirits? Is it modern plumbing and electric lights? Is it ability to read the newspaper headlines or repeat the catechism? Is it even obedience to the Christian moral code? Or is it faith in Christ? Is it an affirmation by man after man and community after community that Christ is Lord, a cry, "Lord I believe, help Thou my unbelief?"

The theological answer would be: Must we not accustom ourselves to the thought of very large populations of Christians, real Christians, whose standard of living, degree of belief in primitive science (magic), ability to read the Scriptures, and actual apprehension of the mind of Christ leave much room for improvement? Can we not count on the Holy Spirit to operate in their lives? So let them in. If they believe in Christ, belong to His Church and accept the Bible as their Scriptures, they are His. These are the multitudes God has called from the highways and the byways. That is why they have come. Who are you to deny entrance to those whom God has called? He will give them a new white robe. That is not your task. He will go with them. He will guard and illumine them. And when it is His gracious pleasure, He will call them home and judge them.

All five replies warn against permitting the passion for perfection to deflect the Church from discipling populations as they become ready for it.

XIV

"GRADUALISM"

"Gradualism" holds that churchmen should carry on activities which so change men that after many years they will be able to embrace the Christian faith. Since practically all populations are initially irresponsive and many remain so for decades and perhaps centuries, this is a doctrine on which much church and mission work starts and continues. It tries to prepare populations for later decision.

A missionary was assigned some years ago to a church of 240 members and a mission high school of 14 Christian and 197 non-Christian boys. He earnestly hoped that some of the 197 would accept Christ as Saviour. He taught classes in the Bible every day. Prior to his arrival, for over fifteen years no baptisms from the world had occurred in this city. His own experience with his students too helped convince him that social and religious pressures effectively blocked any but a very occasional conversion. Consequently he redefined his task as providing his students with the best possible education shot through and through with Christian principles and ideals. He expected this would free their minds, breaking down their prejudices, create an appreciation of Christ, and thus prepare for later harvest. "The sons and grandsons of my students," he would say, "will be free to become Christians." He was practising "gradualism."

An entire mission among unresponsive men and women spent fifty years and $3,000,000. At the end of that time it had twelve congregations totalling 2,845 communicant members. At the jubilee a speaker, lifted to heights of enthusiasm by the occasion, ventured the prophecy that the next fifty years would see another dozen congregations established with a total communicant membership, he hoped, of 5,000. He was applauded. This entire mission was in the grip of "gradualism."

Recently in Egypt the government ruled that all schools must teach the Koran. Christian schools had to decide whether to close, or teach the Koran and continue. Most of them decided to teach the Koran. They thought that it was better to maintain schools which brought Muslim youth into friendly contact with Christianity than to close the schools entirely. "This," they said, "is small return now. Yet serving Egypt in the name of Christ is a witness. Given time it will bear fruit. The intense antipathy to Christianity born of centuries of warfare will yield to kindness and service. If this must be centuries long, we must continue it." This is "gradualism."

An able churchman, trained in sociology and agriculture, was sent to an area where there were no Christians whatever. As he studied his people, he found that the ancient culture of the villages was in process of decay. Invaded by the urban culture of a nearby city it was suffering a series of defeats. Its educated younger leadership, finding no incentive, spiritual or material, to stay in the villages, was leaving. Its religious centres failed to meet the challenge of the new day. The churchman threw himself into a programme of rural reconstruction with practically no preaching or inviting people to become disciples of Christ. Training the youth for community enterprises, encouraging the temples to serve the people, providing recreation for children, instituting co-operative societies for marketing and credit, and being a friend to all, consumed his days and nights. In five years about a dozen youths of the mission school had become Christian. He counted on these becoming leaders of the cultural revival of the countryside. "As this fine old rural culture is preserved against the inroads of urbanism," he would say, "it will be found that the best leaders are those who receive spiritual strength from Jesus Christ. Thus in a quiet way Christianity will be accepted as the form of religion which actually makes life most abundant. Antagonism to Christianity arises when men regard it as an alien culture forcing its way in. In my strategy, Christianity will appear as a spiritual power serving to make abundant life possible. Of course," he explained, "we must continue this programme for many years before we can count on any considerable church growth."

"Gradualism" does something else *now*—some good Christian

activity—that church growth may occur *later*. Congregations are now consolidating their position so that later on great growth can take place. Missionaries are learning the cultural and religious pattern so that later on they can talk to men about the Saviour. The churchman will give direct open witness to his Lord after he gets through his present job. The churchwoman is going to speak to neighbours about the Saviour after her family grows up. The principal's regular duties fill his days, but he expects that in some years grateful ex-students will return asking to be introduced to Jesus Christ. The doctor heals in the hope that, in the future, former patients will seek out the Great Physician.

Sometimes "gradualism" has been the only kind of mission possible. For example, in some sections of Africa 100 years ago, missions faced such complete rejection that the only way they could get a Christian community was to buy slaves and then free and settle them at mission stations. The Lutherans in Liberia took 40 boys and 40 girls off a captured slaver and settled them on a square mile of jungle. Sierra Leone arose as a colony for released slaves.

Sometimes "gradualism" seems the only possibility today too—as in Arabia and Morocco.

The practical questions facing those who carry on this limited Christian witness (sometimes not mentioning the name of Christ) are these: Are we preaching the Gospel openly enough so that men have a real chance to know the Saviour? Is there reasonable hope that our plough is genuinely preparing the soil, or is it sliding to and fro on the surface of a rock? Is there a justified hope that during the coming fifty years our programme will pass from ploughing to sowing, to weeding, to reaping, in orderly sequence? If not, are there populations of winnable people in the world, not now being won, where we could work? What answer shall we give the Lord for failing to harvest those whom He has prepared while cultivating a field the date of whose ripening we cannot even guess?

Often "gradualism" is no longer necessary and yet carries on by its own momentum. Thus the educational missionary of our first illustration, who was expecting his labours to bear fruit in the sons and grandsons of his students, ignored or simply failed to seize opportunities for winning people in his district. Enmeshed in unnecessary "gradualism" he did not even recognize them.

In Puerto Rico a Methodist minister said, "We built up a small congregation of about sixty communicant members in an important town and then, being convinced that we had won about all who could be won there, set ourselves to the nurture of our Christians and the service of the community. We believed that as this process went on for a few decades, a more liberal attitude would result among the people of the world and our church would grow again. However, we had barely started this new programme before the Assemblies of God arrived and, not knowing that we had won all the winnable people in town, built up from the world a membership of over 150 communicants!" The Methodists in that town had settled for "gradualism" unnecessarily.

Unnecessary "gradualism" underlies many missions and younger church practices in many lands. It is persistence in siege tactics after a wall has fallen. It is a well feathered young bird imagining it cannot fly. It is enchainment to a rocky field when strawberries have ripened in the adjoining meadow.

Tomorrow, "gradualism" will be even less necessary than it is today. As more and more fields ripen, there will be less and less reason for it. As indigenous Churches multiply (such as the Little Flock in Formosa, the *Iglesia Ni Christo* in the Philippines, the African Independent Churches and many others), mighty united Churches press forward combining the resources of national and missionary leadership, and revolutions loosen the cement in which men's minds have set, there will be less and less need for "gradualism." We are not perturbed when it is really the only possible way: we are perturbed when it is unnecessary.

There is no instance of "gradualism" in the New Testament. The early evangelists never settled into some place hoping by their own labours to ripen it, after which men would be converted. They went to communities which were ripened by God and worked and prayed for conversion. They expected churches to arise. As far as the record runs they did not remain to labour where the Gospel was not obeyed.

The command of our Lord was clear. "The harvest is plentiful, but the labourers are few. . . . Go . . . If anyone will not receive you, shake off the dust of your feet as you leave that house or town." This is no chance remark. In the immensely important matter of spreading the news of the Kingdom and winning disciples, these words underscored the essentials. There was no time to waste on Gospel rejectors. The harvest was plentiful. The task was to find the responsive houses and towns and bear witness to them.

This command was understood and treasured by the early Church. That is why it is recorded by Matthew, Mark and Luke. It was a principle of action used again and again during the first fifty years of church expansion. Barnabas and Paul shook off the dust of their feet against Antioch and went on to Iconium. Jesus' words must frequently have guided them where not to stay and, indeed, where not to go. The choice then, like that in many places today, had continually to be made between bearing witness where people would not obey and building congregations where they would. Both could not be done. Inexorable choices stared men in the face. "Go to where congregations can be built" was the marching order for the New Testament Church. That is why it is in the record.

"Gradual" mission and church work cannot escape the gaze of two groups of men. (*a*) Hundreds of thousands, who can be discipled this year and every succeeding year for the foreseeable future. Winnable multitudes waiting to be won. Populations large and small, intelligentsia and peasantry, individuals and groups, men and women—all on the march. (*b*) Millions from among whom, no matter how evangelistically and institutionally Christ is proclaimed, only a handful will follow Him this year or any succeeding year for the foreseeable future. "Gradualism" faces the inexorable choice; if it spends men and money in preparatory practices among the millions of Gospel rejectors, hundreds of thousands of would-be Gospel acceptors will die without accepting the Saviour. The men and women now practising "gradualism" must live with the question: Shall we by-pass those who can now be saved in order to do vaguely preparatory work among those who cannot? The theological implications of the answer are enormous.

"Gradualism" has served a purpose. Ploughing generally precedes reaping. The trouble does not lie in that undisputed fact. It lies in the equally undisputed fact that preoccupation with ploughing regularly by-passes opportunities for reaping.

"Gradualism" believes that what the Church or mission does by way of preparation is the determinative factor in ripening. It believes that a Church or mission can choose a population—students, intelligentsia, citizens of this district or peasants of that—and by its efforts cause that particular population to ripen. The churchman in our first illustration believed that the Christian education given in his school would, over a generation or two, create a community of *graduates of his school* from which the Church would grow. The evidence does not support this belief. Ripening is caused by many factors—changes in national destiny, the wish of Christians, upsurges and downswings in the total outlook, the fulness of time, and the providence of God. When the Prophet Harris of Liberia swept across the Ivory Coast in 1914 he found a great population, among whom no missionary had laboured, prepared by the psychological, tribal, political, and military currents of West Africa. He baptized scores of thousands, told them to build chapels and buy Bibles (which they could not read), and wait the coming of teachers. Then he went back to Liberia! There was, unavoidably, wastage. But ten years later when the missionaries found them, there were still 20,000 faithful. In Formosa today the ripeness of the Mandarin-speaking Mainlanders and the Malayan-tongued Highlanders was caused by such things as the Japanese dream of a Japanized South-East Asia, World War II, the rise of Communism, and the defeat of the Chinese nationalism. Vigorous Christian work amongst the ripened populations is gathering great harvest.

Churches should regard all "gradual" enterprises as watch towers from which to observe where church growth can take place and from which to shift resources into direct multiplication of congregations. "If the field I am ploughing does not ripen," says the wise churchman, "while another does, I shall turn the ploughing over to my third son, take the two big boys and go over to help bring in the sheaves—before it rains!"

XV

THE PRISON OF PREVIOUS PATTERNS

In the year A.D. 48 the young Church found itself imprisoned. Its hugely successful pattern of expansion had been to identify the Church with Israel, Jesus Christ with the expected Messiah, and "to speak the word to none but Jews." It thus rode the strong current of Jewish faith. Jews joined the Christian Church as Jews. They continued observing the Sabbath and Jewish feasts, worshipping in the temple, and refraining from the use of pork. The expansion of the Church strictly within the Jewish race as a part of Judaism for fifteen crucial years deprived the Pharisees of the deadly weapon which they would have had if they had been able to claim that to become a Christian was to become a Gentile.

But when at Antioch there was visible—at first to the eye of faith only—a great new field in the Gentile sympathizers in the synagogue communities around the Mediterranean, the exclusively Jewish pattern became a prison. Continued identification of the Church with "none but Jews" would have kept it from reaping a ripened harvest of Jewish sympathizers and Gentile friends. God revealed to Peter that the pattern was not His will. Paul devoted himself to breaking it into pieces.

That first pattern was composed of racial prejudices interwoven with doctrines about the nature of God, man and salvation. Patterns today are made up of organization and method.

(1) For example, here is a younger Church of 20,000 communicant members. Its hugely successful pattern has been to appoint a village catechist, largely on mission funds, for every new congregation established, and to expect that with the passage of the years these congregations of 100 to 150 communicants would become more and more self-supporting. As is always the case, there comes a time when the development of self-support in such churches becomes acutely necessary. Perhaps there has been a fall in the rate of exchange so that the pound brings fewer yen. Perhaps a depres-

sion has swept the sending country. Perhaps better educated pastors demand more salary. Whatever it is, the leaders of the Church talk the problem out and decide to put all churches on complete self-support. No subsidy! Salary scales are made out, churches assessed, prayer offered to God, courage screwed up and the pattern is outlined. Some pastors quit: their places are filled. Some churches baulk! They are visited and persuaded. The new pattern has its ups and downs. There are more victories than defeats. Every nerve is strained to make it work.

At just this juncture a new segment of the population becomes winnable. News comes that churches can be established. Inquirers are coming every week. Requests for meetings, for catechists, for baptism are reported, not in great profusion but enough to make it clear that if catechists on half subsidy are provided, very considerable ingathering will occur. If, however, no subsidy at all is given and men are not baptized unless they will fully support a catechist, new churches will not come into existence. Facing this dilemma, the existing Church meets. "How can we give them catechists on half subsidy, when our older churches are getting none," says one. "The whole subsidy business is a bad thing," exclaims another. "But," objects a third, "these men at the beginning of their Christian life are willing to pay half of their catechist's salary. Remember, our present churches started out with full subsidy. I think we should take them in." Finally, the chairman sums up the sense of the meeting and says, "If they will fully support a catechist from the beginning, we'll press the extension of the Church among them; otherwise not." The pattern of the existing Church has become a prison.

(2) The exploratory pattern also can become a prison-house. When missions approach untouched districts, they meet much opposition and misunderstanding and have no way to tell what sections of the population will accept Christ. They set up a pattern of good works of education and medicine to convince people of their genuine friendliness, and much evangelism to tell the good news of salvation. Now as this exploratory pattern continues from decade to decade it becomes a prison-house. The patterns must be followed. If converts come where work is being done, excellent. The school man will care for the spiritual nurture of those of his students who seek

Christ. The doctors will work with those who come in through the hospital, the evangelist with those who come in through wide-spread preaching. But if some great opportunity for increase comes outside the pattern, it is usually lost. The exploratory pattern becomes a prison.

(3) A maturing Church is caught up in the transfer of authority to nationals. All arguments are mustered in its favour. It engages the enthusiasm of the churchmen working it. Constitutions are written and new organizational forms worked out. For the Church to be fully in control is accepted as wholly desirable. New missionaries are trained in the new order. A new vocabulary is worked out—missionaries become fraternal workers, missions become inter-church aid. Every nerve is strained to make the new pattern work.

Then some colossal opening occurs to which the younger Church is blind. The assisting mission also, shrinking from any action which might appear to dominate, turns a deaf ear to the muffled cries of inarticulate multitudes groping for the Saviour. The necessary pattern of complete national control has proved a prison-house for the expansion of the Church.

Stanley Jones in *The Christ of the Indian Road* declared Western Christianity to be for India an imprisoning pattern and insisted that an Indian pattern with Christ at its centre could be much more readily accepted by Indians. The Christian Movement is deeply indebted to Dr Jones for this insight which applies not only to India but to every land. In this chapter we carry the thought a step further and point out that within one nation or one country there are numerous patterns, each suited to its own patch of population and its own times, and each by virtue of that very fact likely to become a prison-house, preventing extension of the churches in other groupings of people and other times.

Each pattern assumes that as its various parts prosper, the Church will, of course, grow and men will, of course, be converted. That is why the parts have been set up. That is why "they spake the word to none but Jews." That is why departments of work were set up. But the time comes when the parts are reinforced and continued, whether the Church grows or not.

What is the remedy?

We turn to the Scriptures. What enabled the Church to break

out of its prison in the year of our Lord 48? It was men led of the Holy Spirit—a Cyprian Jew named Barnabas and Saul of Tarsus. These men had convictions. They believed that winnable people anywhere were vastly more important than the racial pattern of the first two decades. "If the pattern keeps men from salvation," they said, "the pattern must go." These words are not found in the New Testament, but heroic lives through the years have testified to it. Paul's decision was a costly one. It involved constant misunderstanding with the leaders of the Church. It made Paul a lone apostle—and lonely too in his relation with the leader of the Jewish section of the early Church. It brought him ridicule and rejection. In practically every town he visited, not only were the strict Jews his mortal enemies, but his Christian brothers of the strict Jewish persuasion were quite sure he was wrong, and in many places sought to undo his work and discredit him.

The decision that the Gentiles were winnable and that the old pattern must be broken required courage. It had to be taken at Antioch *before* the first missionary journey was made. The Gentiles might not prove winnable. "Maybe other synagogue communities will obey the Gospel as that in Antioch has, and maybe they won't. Antioch may be an exception"—thoughts like these ran through the mind of Barnabas and Saul. Like all opportunities for church growth, that in the synagogue communities rose over the horizon with no guarantee on it. It was an untried field. The Gentiles in large numbers had never been won before. No missionaries today anywhere in the world can possibly experience a greater departure into the unknown than these two did. But Barnabas and Saul decided to break the old pattern, to baptize the Gentiles without circumcising them, before the conversions of the first missionary journey had taken place, and while the Jerusalem Council's decision was yet unknown. That took courage.

As we observe Paul breaking the pattern we can see the part played in it by his spiritual experiences. "Not I but Christ," he says. "My judgements as a Christian Jew would be something entirely different. The Jewish pattern of Christianity under which I was baptized by a brother Jew and under which I lived for many years would lead me to one set of decisions concerning you Gentiles. But I have died. What lives in me is Christ who came to save sinners—

Paul the sinner, Jewish sinners, Gentile sinners. All have sinned and come short of the glory of God. So I now work under a new pattern as inclusive as the love of God itself. It is not my wisdom—that would reject you. It is not my convenience—that would have kept me in Tarsus. It is certainly not the judgement of my senior colleagues specially the Reverend S. Peter, Reverend J. B. Zebedee and Reverend James Joseph. But it is Christ's will. I cannot go contrary to that."

Some such process broke the pattern in the year 48. It has broken imprisoning patterns down through the ages, and it is breaking them today. There must always be a man who breaks imprisoning patterns. Like Paul he usually has intense concern that men accept Christ as Saviour. This, not the accustomed way of doing things, the Church customs, the mission pattern, is of primary importance in his eyes.

Like Paul on his first missionary journey, he makes a venture of faith: church growth is never a certainty. To break with imprisoning patterns before knowing that the opportunity will certainly yield new churches takes courage, imagination and faith. It involves loneliness and misunderstanding and many an hour of inner uncertainty when the man questions whether he is right. Yet it is the chief way in which new varieties of vigorous church growth begin.

XVI

PERMANENT *v.* PAULINE INVOLVEMENT

The length of involvement of the mission with the young Church is one of the most important factors affecting church growth. Modern missions are finding themselves permanently involved with the Churches they establish at ever greater cost to the sending Churches. First they are there as missions during a period of fifty to a hundred years. Then they are there as partners during a long period of devolution. Finally, they are there on a permanent subsidy with increasingly less voice in management. Often, through these three stages, the resources involved do not wane, but wax. In the final stage any hint that funds may be reduced is taken as an infringement of the rights of the younger Church and regarded as economic control. More and more, "missions" come to mean permanent involvement.

Even when the Churches themselves become largely self-supporting, involvement continues because the auxiliary services—schools, hospitals, agricultural institutes, colleges, universities—require ever-increasing sums of assistance from abroad. Freed in one sphere, the attachment becomes closer than ever in another.

Since the younger Churches and their fields of labour are so large, it may be argued that this permanent involvement is a good thing. However, it is being seen today as never before that permanent assistance is almost impossible to separate from permanent control, which is increasingly resented by those receiving the aid. Control is not the purpose for which aid is given. Indeed, never in the history of the world has so much aid been given with such sincere effort to avoid control. Yet control inheres in aid. It cannot successfully be divorced from it.

To meet this problem, it is proposed that instead of Presbyterian Church A giving missionary assistance of £100,000 to Presbyterian

Church S on the other side of the world (which has the disadvantage that Church S feels resentment at the veiled control held by Church A) Church A and Church S should both contribute to a World Fund of Inter-Church Aid. This *World Body* on which S was represented would then spend the Fund to which S had contributed £1,000 and was entitled by right, not by grace. The plan may have some advantages. It adds one link to the chain. Yet when Church S knows that its founding Church A is putting £100,000 into the World Fund and that S will continue to receive something in the neighbourhood of £100,000 only as long as A continues to put it in, will not economic control still be in operation? And still, despite the most Christian intentions on both sides, generate a degree of resentment?

When we turn to New Testament Missions we find a totally different picture. Involvement was exceedingly temporary. Paul came, stayed a few weeks or months or at most a few years, and left to go elsewhere and plant other churches. The churches he planted did not remain in his control. There was constant danger, as the letter to the churches in Galatia indicates, that they would even depart from his fundamental teaching. He would exhort them not to do so, but he had no funds which he could cut off to prevent them doing so. They were free. The modern picture must be seen against the Pauline background. Modern missions may be right. They may be wrong. But they are certainly different from Pauline missions. They are launched and continued in the expectation of permanent involvement growing ever more and more expensive.

There are, however, two significant exceptions to this generalization. First, where whole countrysides have become Christian modern missions have often followed the Pauline pattern, at least *for rural Christians*. In the country congregations, the contact of the missionary has been temporary and has grown less and less with the passage of the years. He has established the churches and passed on. Today's country congregations seldom see a white man. Their pastors are nationals, their supervisors are nationals, and what they get for the expense of the local churches is what they themselves raise. One thinks at once of the great Anglican Church of Uganda, the Baptist Church in rural Burma, the Lutheran Churches in South India and New Guinea. The initial period of involvement was longer than that of Paul's, but the turnover in the villages has been quite as complete.

Second, where war or tyranny has driven out the missionary and permanent endowment from the West, there involvement has been terminated. The Lutheran Church in Chhota Nagpur, India, was run through the wringer twice—once in World War I when its founding German missionaries were banished from India, and again during World War II. The World Lutheran Federation is concurrently helping this great Church of over 150,000 souls with a small grant—possibly $60,000 a year, but for many years aid from the West was very small. The great Batak Church of North Sumatra, now numbering 650,000 souls, for many years was staffed by only twenty-five missionaries, during World War II had none, and in 1956 had less than a dozen. In China we have seen a tremendous forced weaning. The essential Church not only survived, but, till the active persecution of 1958, prospered. Had anyone suggested to Christian Missions in China in 1940 that they terminate their relationship with their established congregations, he would have been considered a fool or an enemy of the cause. Yet within ten years a total divorce had been effected—not only from missionaries but from western money—and the Church survived and apparently flourished.

The Pauline pattern and these two significant exceptions force those responsible for modern mission policy to ask: "Are we correct in deliberately planning for permanent involvement? Or, if we are not deliberately planning for it, but have slipped into it unawares, would it not be well to attempt a planned termination of the giving-receiving relationship? If it was broken in these instances, can it not be broken elsewhere with advantage?"

It is most difficult to break this giving and receiving tradition because, in the first place, the younger Churches will not relinquish for themselves the rich services provided by continuing aid. Take almost any younger Church, with its assisting mission, and the picture is one of organizations, men, women, churches, boys and girls—all dependent in greater or less degree for their livelihood, education, hope and happiness on large grants from abroad. Such grants seem absolutely essential to the continued life of the Church. All the pressure is to increase not diminish them. Even greater grants could be used profitably. It seems absolutely impossible to cut them off. To do so appears certain to crush many fine men and women and possibly to spark a great outburst of resentment.

When some outside agency, like war or tyranny, cuts off this life-line, the Church, feeling no anger against its founding fathers, makes the adjustment. This is a historic fact and has occurred again and again. But whether the adjustment could be made by a Church which knew that its founding fathers and assisting sisters, though amply able to continue aid for years, had deliberately cut off assistance—that is another question.

In the second place it is difficult to break this tradition, because the older Churches have not thought out what *a valid Church in a population of far less privilege involves*. If the older Churches have to choose between (*a*) continued assistance to a discipled population with an average *per capita* income of $100 a year, and (*b*) discipling other such populations, they will choose the former. They choose it because they vaguely feel that there cannot be a valid or an effective Church in a low-income population. They feel that the only way to obtain a valid Church is to pour in foreign funds so that the Christians are lifted far above what would otherwise be their lot. The Western Churches are not content to leave younger Churches with merely the Bible, the Church, the Holy Spirit, and faith in the Lord. Until they become literate how can they know anything about the Bible? Until they produce much more rice how can they possibly support a respectable pastor? Until they have high schools, colleges, and theological seminaries—to take advantage of which they need large subsidies—how can they possibly have a trained ministry? These are the considerations which lead the older Churches to continue large amounts of aid to even well established Churches.

Yet, on the other hand, when war and tyranny have once broken the bond, we see the older Churches re-establishing with pride relationship with younger Churches like that of Chhota Nagpur, or the Ewe Presbyterian Church in Ghana, which have stabilized themselves at a much lower level than their founding missions would ever have considered decent. And where whole countrysides have become Christian, as in sections of the Cameroons, South India, or Samoa, the older and younger Churches regard the country congregations, which exist at that low economic level, as valid Church-members even though regrettably under-privileged.

In the third place, as a continuing process, permanent involvement is difficult to break because the younger Churches themselves are not clear on what constitutes good mission policy. Here is Church A of 100,000 communicants in Korea or the Philippines. What constitutes good mission policy for it as it sends missionaries to Thailand? Is it to try to meet Thailand's needs—to make available to that great land the best that Church A has to offer; to study Buddhism, the national religion of Thailand, and work out such a statement of Christianity as shall bring Buddhists gladly to accept the Saviour as the crown of Buddhism; to establish great educational centres through which Buddhists will become modern men of good will, inheritors of the vast knowledge now available to Church A; to pioneer medical centres, leprosy homes, literacy campaigns, and make them over to government as fast as it is able to manage them; go on to new enterprises for the welfare of Thailand; and to preach Christ so that men will know that all Church A does is inspired by Him? If this is the answer, then Church A is in for permanent involvement—growing more and more expensive year by year.

Or is it good mission policy to found congregations of believers, assist them to found others, leave them to work out a Thai adjustment to Thai culture, let the congregations have on the whole about as much education as Thailand gives its citizens plus what the churches themselves can give, make available some aid in training of the ministry, and, having done this, to pass on to other sections of Thailand and elsewhere to plant other congregations? If this is the answer, Church A is in for temporary involvement.

By-and-large, the world mission of the Church, except where, by depressions, wars, and tyranny, it has been forced out, has acted as if it considered that a valid Church and sound mission policy among low income groups required permanent assistance. Thus world evangelization is grievously slowed down at this point. Most of its resources are tied up with existing little growing Churches.

Evidence shows that greatly aided churches do not grow greatly. There is seldom positive correlation between degree of aid and amount of growth. Aid under some circumstances does produce growth, but a vast amount of aid can be poured out for decades with inconsiderable growth.

This situation unless corrected will grow worse and worse. Every time a new mission is created by older or younger Churches, that mission enters into a permanent involvement growing annually more expensive. Practically none of the present elaborate organizational arrangements for enhancing the independent status of younger Churches is of any avail because these arrangements concern themselves solely with political and psychological independence and studiously avoid any hint of financial independence.

Yet the picture is not all dark. The gleams of light shine precisely in those younger Churches which by war, tyranny, or depression have been forced into complete independence. Instead of regarding them as tragedies in the evangelization of the world, the world mission should regard them as pioneers in the process of disentanglement. The world mission should now enter upon an era of planned weaning. This will proceed at different rates of speed and different methods of implementation for each homogeneous unit. There will be no uniform procedure. However, certain principles will guide.

(1) Maturity will be defined as being completely self-supporting, self-governing and self-propagating, and contributing a reasonable proportion to world evangelization. The contribution may be through a common pool or may be direct. Maturity will mean stabilization at whatever level the general income of the country concerned permits. This may mean, as in the Church of South India, that the ordained ministers supported by the Church will be supplemented by ordained ministers who earn their own living at other jobs. The world mission will not say, "A good Christian programme demands xyz. If Church A can provide this programme with its local resources it will be counted mature; otherwise we shall continue indefinitely to aid it." Instead the world mission will say, "What a mature Christian programme is considered to be has depended in every century of the Church on local conditions. What a Church is able to do of itself, on the basis of sturdy self-sufficiency, without the artificial standards made possible by long continued foreign subsidy,

is much better for a Church than any programme judged adequate by highly privileged foreign Christians."

(2) The missionary task will include not merely establishing the Church, but leaving it. National leaders, planning for the maturity of the younger Churches, will draw up time-tables indicating when financial involvement with the older Churches, in any shape or form, shall be methodically reduced and at a given point finally terminated. There certainly will not be a general time-table for the Churches in any given land. Thus, in the United Church of Christ in the Philippines, there may be one time-table for the Church in Manila, another for that in Mindanao, and still another for that in Apayao. In some, the time-table will call for increased foreign aid. In others it will call for decreased or terminated foreign aid.

(3) Within the time-limits set for complete termination of foreign aid, attention will be focused on the following essential tasks:

(*a*) Training a pastorate to care for the local congregations, to be a link with the world Church, and to ensure reproduction and self-propagation—all completely supported by the younger Church.

(*b*) Working out an organization necessary to survival. Each homogeneous unit Church—be it one of 1,000 or 50,000 communicant members—either across denominational boundaries or within them—needs to be built into a larger unit.

(*c*) Setting up patterns of Christian life—worship, community responsibility, tithing, marriage, spiritual living, and the like.

(*d*) Lifting the general level of health and education as far as possible—recognizing that to lift it artificially high with foreign resources, which are going to terminate, may actually do the community a disservice.

(4) When the time-limit approaches, aid will be methodically withdrawn and invested immediately in planting homogeneous Churches elsewhere.

In short, what Paul did by conviction, what the Batak, Uraon, Munda, and Chinese Churches have been forced to do by war and tyranny, what the Church in Uganda and others like it have done by virtue of the enormous numbers they have won, and what every Church with large numbers of rural congregations today automatically does, Churches and missions must do as a planned policy. Only this process will restore to the Churches the resources they must have for total evangelization.

These principles apply to mature younger Churches of whatever size just as truly as to older Churches. For example, there are dozens of missionary societies maintained by the younger Churches in India. Each one of them is in danger of permanent involvement with *its* younger Church! The missionary society of each younger Church, therefore, facing its own task, sets itself to bring into existence not a permanent dependency but a truly self-supporting, self-governing and self-propagating Church of Christ.

As resources are withdrawn from sister Churches so that they may enjoy sturdy independence, what happens to the central continuing mission of the Church—the total evangelization of the world? Are resources re-invested independently by the sending Churches (be they Eastern or Western) in some unoccupied field? Are they invested in outreach in co-operation with those of the national Churches? Are they withdrawn from Churches which have reached not only maturity but also a dead-end to expansion, and invested with other Churches which have great potential growth? These questions cannot be answered "in general." They must be answered for specific Churches in specific populations.

The ripe fields next to established Churches are ready and waiting for joint teams representing national and foreign Churches. Thus in Sarguja, which lies next to Chhota Nagpur, a joint effort by the Gossner Evangelical Lutheran Church of 200,000 and World Lutheran Federation was natural. The united effort was much more effective than any separate effort could possibly have been.

Where ripe fields lie at a distance, there may still be room for missionary effort by the world Church entirely independent of the national Churches. A good many opportunities may open up where a national Church says, "We already have so many burdens that we cannot assume responsibility for that ripe field. Go in alone and God bless you."

Finally, where the established Church is in the midst of such a ripe field that many of its congregations simply reach out where they are and bring their neighbours to Christ, it may be difficult to withdraw and re-invest resources, because that would mean withdrawal from a rapidly expanding Church. What better field could the mission find than the responsive one which exists inter-twined with the established Church? Perhaps the question of withdrawing resources need not arise as long as any homogeneous unit is increasing at 100 per cent, or more. This could only be true for homogeneous units. Otherwise, as in Church X of Indofrica described in Chapter 4, where such a condition might be true for unit AB, large forces could be tied up in permanent involvement with non-growing units C and D.

The continued growth of the Church depends in considerable measure on successful achievement by its younger Churches of a really independent status. That such status can be achieved the entire course of church history attests. That it can be achieved today, even under very difficult circumstances, is proven by modern cases we have quoted. It remains for Churches to become independent, or at least to press forward to independence as a natural, desirable, and inevitable goal.

The time-table will vary for each homogeneous unit. The temptation will be strong to defer cutting the apron strings for a long time—or to deny that the strings are there. When the founded Churches accept genuine independence as a desirable goal and press toward it *themselves*, possibly in advance of the schedule thought wise by the founding Churches, the best results may be hoped for. In some cases the founding Church may have to take the initiative, work out a framework which can continue when mission aid is withdrawn, and then gently push the founded Church on to it. Permanent and increasingly expensive involvement successfully stops expansion, and therefore in one way or another it must be terminated. It must give way to some variety of temporary involvement resulting in really independent Churches.

PART IV

METHODS OF CHURCH-GROWTH

XVII

METHODS WHICH MULTIPLY CHURCHES

Manati is a small town on the north shore of Puerto Rico. Its citizens—who are also citizens of the United States—are middle-class Latins with many years of compulsory education behind them. Merchants, factory owners, factory workers, teachers, clerks, small business men, government servants of one sort and another, and retired people, make up the population. The Christian Church in Manati numbered 107 communicant members in 1948. Six years later its membership stood at 220. This growth, at the rate of about 200 per cent per decade, was matched by several metropolitan Christian Churches, but no other small town Church had anything approaching this rate of growth. Indeed, most of them showed a mere 10 to 20 per cent.

When asked, "What makes your church grow," the deacons and elders said:

> Everyone in this congregation prays all year long by name for some friend or loved one that he may be saved. Then before our annual week of meetings the congregation assembles to write these names on the board and to pray unitedly for them. During this week of meetings from thirty to eighty men, women, and young people from the world are converted and added to the church. That is how it happens. We ask God for them. God answers our prayers.

Church growth does not "just happen" anywhere. It is not the happy coincidence of finding a suitable people and reaping a rich harvest. Church growth occurs when Christians work hard among a suitably responsive people. The Baptist mission among the Karens in Burma has been called "the most successful mission of them all." The Church started in 1827. By 1842 it numbered about

5,000 members and by 1942 over 200,000. This is great growth. What made it grow?

The answer is: the hardest kind of labour in the most impossible surroundings. Karen evangelists and missionaries travelled along jungle trails in constant danger from wild animals and disease. Where there was no path through the forest they waded along a stream. They crossed steep mountains in order to reach distant villages. Often they were refused entrance to villages. Political resentment at the progress of Christianity mounted, and Judson was imprisoned for months; but the work of discipling the Karens went on.

After churches had been started, Christians continued to work to increase them. Revival meetings were held and were continued for weeks with no seeming response. Then the dam would break and members would pour in. The veteran missionaries triumphed over great difficulties. Karens did not easily become Christians. The Church cost sweat, toil, tears and blood.

In Belgian Congo I was discussing church growth with a friendly and highly placed Roman Catholic prelate. Among factors which prevented church growth he named "American cars." "What on earth do you mean?" I asked. He answered:

> The priests who are not securing growth are those who buzz out in a car to say Mass or solve some problem and buzz back in again. But where the priest sets out on foot, makes a village a day, is accessible to the people all day long, sleeps there at night, comes to know his people, and returns two or three weeks later—there the church is growing greatly. Footwork and sweat are involved.

A triumphant example of church growth today comes from Japan from amongst a cosmopolitan, highly educated population which has not in general yielded much fruit. The Oriental Missionary Society, going back to Japan after the war, found that twelve of its former congregations had come out of the United Church into which they had been forced by the government in 1941. They wanted the assistance of the Oriental Missionary Society in nurturing and extending their Church. The Church of twelve congregations in 1948 had by December 1955 become a Church of 84 congregations of which each had a resident pastor, 44 paid their pastors' entire salary from the congregation's contributions only, 40 paid their pastors from congregational contributions plus some mission subsidy, 34 had built or were building chapels at their own expense, and 50 were meeting in rented quarters. How did this extraordinary growth come about? I was told:

> A theological seminary and three tent-teams comprise our chief method. We have eighteen instructors in the seminary, some of whom give part time only. Seventy young men and women comprise the student body. They are engaged in a three-year course. Twenty more are enrolled in night courses. The academic qualification for entrance into the regular course is a high-school diploma. The seminary prepares our pastors.
>
> We use about twenty Japanese and six Americans in the three tent-teams. Each team has a truck, a big tent, and the equipment needed to hold a meeting anywhere, and each team has about seven Japanese, who do most of the speaking, and two Americans. We pray for guidance as to where to send the teams. They preach Christ night after night in town or suburb for a few weeks till enough people are converted to start a congregation. One recent tent-meeting of three weeks' duration was held in the courtyard of a temple. Several Buddhists, including a priest, accepted Christ. These, having received baptism, were received into membership in one of our churches.
>
> Our churches are not built up with converts from other denominations. Less than 1 per cent have been students in other mission schools. Ninety per cent at least have little previous knowledge of Christianity. Most of them are under thirty years of age. They include both students and young married couples. These latter, already earning, enable the congregation to be self-supporting. When a new congregation needs further help we go back the next year and hold another meeting.

"What is the most important part of this method?" we asked. "Keeping the teams blessed," came the ready reply.

In a section of India, where the Church is growing at about 200 per cent and about 3,000 baptisms from the world have occurred in the last four years, a campaign by word of mouth commonly called "spontaneous evangelism by laymen" is a prominent method of church-growth. In constant conversations with their relatives in home, field, and market-place, Christians unconsciously tell of a superior kind of life and their relatives unconsciously come to desire it. Drop in to any of the several hundred Christian groups scattered across the villages of the plain and ask, "What are your kinsman thinking about Christianity?" They will answer like this:

> "I was talking to my relatives in Puddumpur four months ago. They were ready to become Christian." "If I were to spend a month with my mother's brother, I think they would all become Christian. They like our religion and often stop here on their way to market." "My sister married before our family became Christian. Her husband recently went to Calcutta to work. He told her to attend church regularly pending his return when his whole family of twenty-five would become Christian." "My cousins believe that Christianity is a superior way of life. They note that evil spirits do not trouble us and that we treat our women folk better than they do." "My wife's father says that there is no book like the Bible and that in a year or two he and his son and their families will join us."

This campaign by word of mouth had by 1920 created a widespread willingness to espouse the Christian religion. From that time to this, the rate of church growth has depended solely on the degree to which churchmen reached out. When they did, they found a harvest ready to reap. The unconscious persuading had been going on quietly for years in the hearts of the people. The reaching out is therefore successful.

One of the modern cities of Latin America is San Juan in Puerto, with its paved streets, electric lights, and modern sanitation. Cash registers ring in the stores and adding machines clatter in the offices. Modern schools teach tens of thousands of boys and girls. Business men in Western dress engage in all the various pursuits of modern man. The university brings the rich cosmopolitan culture of the twentieth century to large numbers of choice students.

In the midst of this city is a Christian Church which, starting in 1943 with a dozen members, now numbers over 600. What method caused this growth? "Conversion from the world," answers the pastor. "This congregation has some who became Christians elsewhere, moved to San Juan and joined this church. But most of our members are converts." "How do you get in touch with them?"

> We assign all our members to "upper rooms" which are really branch churches, meeting separately in twelve homes for Bible-study and worship under lay leadership during the week, and meeting together at the church on Sunday. Christians in each "upper room" invite their friends to these neighbourhood meetings. Many visitors like the Christian warmth, Bible-study and free worship. They want what these Christians have. They start coming to the Christian Church—which they would have avoided before—and under double instruction from lay Christians and the minister enlist with Christ.

A few years ago, in a responsive caste in India, great growth of the Church was going on. Two methods of harvesting were greatly used by God. These were called after two honoured Indian ministers who had first used them: the Chandra Singh method and the Yohan Prakash method. Chandra Singh preferred a quiet way. He would select promising Christians from new villages, give them a few months' training during the rainy season and then send them to live in friendly villages of this caste. He told them to make themselves one with the people, serve them in every way, instruct those adults who asked for instruction, and teach what children could be gathered together. Usually the villagers gave the teacher a house to live in and, in a course of a few months, he had a group instructed and ready for baptism.

Yohan Prakash preferred an aggressive method. Pastors and laymen from existing congregations would plan a campaign in which a score or more would converge on some village full of their own kith and kin, and there, in a meeting lasting a few days and nights, call on their kinsman to give themselves to God. Those who accepted the Saviour would be baptized and a new congregation started. Each method over a dozen years quadrupled the number of congregations.

In West Nigerian towns the semi-tribal and supra-tribal population is so ready to receive the Gospel that a leading churchman said:

> If we had fifty able preachers we could plant fifty good churches a year. All that is necessary to bring in a self-supporting congregation of 80 to 200 members is to locate a preacher of calibre there. Before the end of the year, there will be a church. He starts visiting and preaching the day he arrives. He continues visiting, teaching, and preaching weekdays and Sundays. Men and women are converted just like they would be in Texas and form congregations which build churches just like they would in Toledo. The response is individual, yet many come in as families. Our task here is to train ministers fast enough.

In Formosa between 1939 and 1945, the method of secret Bible-study prepared 4,000 people for full Christian dedication. The story is this:

> The Highlanders of Formosa are a tough Malayan people. Living in inaccessible mountain fastnesses for centuries they maintained their independence from Chinese and Japanese conquerors. In 1925 they were finally subdued by the Japanese. Scattered schools among them taught some of them to read in Japanese. Practically none had become Christians.
>
> Then about 1930 a lone woman was converted and became a Bible-woman. About 1938 her teaching began to rouse interest in one small section of one small clan. As the coming World War began to influence action, the Japanese forbade this teaching of Christianity. Bible-woman Chi-o-ang could no longer go to interested villages. So those who wanted instruction came to her—at night. They purchased Bibles in Japanese. They started teaching others. In an effort to stamp out "this subversive sect" the Japanese beat, imprisoned, starved, and killed leaders, raided villages for Bibles, and harried the seekers. But secret Bible-study continued in fields and forests and midnight meetings. At the end of the war over 4,000 clansmen came down out of the hills asking for baptism. This started a great discipling which in the last ten years has brought over 50,000 into the Church and is still going on.

Such descriptions could run on for pages and cover only a small part of the methods which multiply churches. They are found in almost every land among every kind of people—educated and illiterate, townsmen and peasants, tribesmen and individuals. They must be seen against the backdrop of a great deal of good work which produces little or no church growth. In the very lands where such ingathering is occurring, many younger Churches and Missions are achieving—and appear satisfied with—church growth of zero to 30 per cent per decade.

Basic to all these methods is a driving concern of some man or woman that others become disciples of the Lord Jesus Christ. This personal burden, like a stream in spate, makes a path for itself. The form of the path—the method—varies as in the previous illustrations according to the circumstances. But back of every method will be found a man who shares Christ's passion for the redemption of men.

In India thirty years ago a unique group of perhaps fifty Indians could have been assembled. These were college graduates who had been converted from the world by one principal of one college. He was a noted educator. He was also intensely concerned that men become Christians.

Thailand is a difficult field where few become Christians and many missionaries spend a lifetime of service and win no one to Christ. But one missionary and wife there, who had carried on schools, hospital, public service, and preaching—the usual thing—had a driving concern that others should accept the Saviour. During thirty years they baptized 367 people from the world. Not many to be sure, but still 367 more than many churchmen have led to Christ. In the same land, a Thai national, converted from nominal Christianity in 1937, by 1956 had personally won over 200 to his Lord.

In another land, where many hospitals were satisfied to be medically competent and kindly, there was one where, year after year, the physician in charge brought to discipleship a stream of persons—not half of them his patients.

A general secretary of a large mission suddenly realized that in many years since his ordination, while he had preached many times, and served his Church and Mission in many capacities, he had not brought a single soul to the feet of the Master. Jarred to action by the realization, he devoted an evening a week to personal evangelism, making time for it in his busy schedule. Nothing happened for three years. He used and discarded six methods of work. While trying the seventh, he had the joy of baptizing nine persons whose coming opened a new door through which over 200 believers have since entered.

The burden must be there. If it is, successful methods will be found.

Successful methods can be classified. First, there are those which operate through church members in the immediate vicinity of the congregations—visitation evangelism, evangelistic campaigns in existing churches, Sunday schools and cottage prayer meetings. These bring converts into existing congregations. New groups start as part of old congregations and continue so until they get big enough to launch out as separate congregations. The instrument of conversion is chiefly the church itself as it witnesses and worships. Members invite their friends to study the Bible in their homes. Bands of laymen go out to teach the Bible regularly in some locality where they think it is needed or believe a church can be established.

Little "Stage One" churches are thus organized—bands of believers and sympathizers who meet regularly to study the Bible, sing and pray, hear preaching, or discuss what God requires of us today. Many "Stage Ones" are born, live a few months or years, and die. But some grow in numbers and become "Stage Twos," where they choose teachers, deacons, and elders from amongst themselves and build themselves a meeting house. They consider themselves a branch of the Mother Church. They continue to receive help and encouragement from it. They do not have a resident pastor. Many Christian groups never get beyond "Stage Two." But some do. Their temporary meeting house becomes a church. They secure a pastor and become "Stage Three" churches. They double and treble their membership. New congregations have been born out of the old ones.

Second, in the classification of successful methods, come those which run ahead of the local congregations. A Filipino layman's business took him across two rivers and up a big hill to two villages where no one had ever become Christian. Some had been baptized in infancy in the Roman Church five miles away but most still bore as a surname the word "infidel"—"Sebastian Infidel." There he visited, held meetings and taught the Bible. He purchased Bibles for the village leaders and helped them in many ways. He thus brought to decision a new segment of society. A missionary in Congo knows that proclamation along a dozen roads where there are no churches will bring streams of decisions. Into the new tribe he goes, ahead of the Church. A cultured Christian in a great Indian city makes his home the meeting-place for non-Christian friends. He pioneers a presentation of Christ, made particularly for that group. From among his visitors a dozen have become disciples of Christ. The Oriental Missionary Society of Japan, with its tent-teams, reaches out beyond its congregations and starts new ones.

A third successful method is that of radio programmes and Bible study courses by mail, which reach both into the ferment on the edges of congregations and into the blue out beyond any known Christian.

What is the relationship between "ripeness" and method? Different answers are required by the three kinds of population. If we distribute populations along a line with the ripest at the right and the unripest at the left, then many methods will serve at the extreme right to harvest churches. There are populations so ripe that individuals constantly seek out Christians, walk miles to worship, and endure persecution that they may know Christ. There are populations so ready to receive the Gospel that "people-movements" take place led by churchmen who are conscientiously opposed to group conversion! "Sirs," all these men are saying, "we would see Jesus."

Among such populations the choice of method is a minor matter. The Nevius[1] method, the Chandra Singh method, the tent-teams, the unpaid witness, the paid leader—all will multiply congregations. But some methods will multiply more than others and some better than others. Some will lead more rapidly to self-support and others will delay it. Some methods appear foreign, generate resistance, or create non-productive churches. Others appear indigenous, generate goodwill, and stamp in patterns possible of indefinite reproduction.

At the left extreme of the distribution are cold populations, so unripe, so satisfied with themselves, so bound by nationalistic or

---

[1] Dr. Nevius was a Presbyterian missionary in Shantung, China. His methods became the working basis of Presbyterian missions in Korea.

tribal prejudices, that no method or combination of methods will now win any appreciable number to Christ. The task there is watching from a chilly outpost for some section of the population to become ripe and responsive. These situations obtain at the two ends of the distribution.

In between, however, is a great spread. In this mid-land, men will become disciples if approached rightly and will remain in the world if they are not. A constellation of Baptist churches, aided by many missionary assistants, stood still for many years with little growth. Then a small group of churchmen, using the method of the band of witness, undergirded with much prayer, started an inflow which added a third to some churches, a half to others, doubled and trebled a few and started some new ones. The Manati church in Puerto Rico harvested in a small town—when in similar small towns none of its sister churches were obtaining any growth! Some churchmen in this middle territory will helplessly wring their hands before the problem of providing pastors for new churches; others will solve the problem and reap an abundant harvest. In this rapidly ripening mid-land, some boards will provide $100,000 for an eye-catching enterprise remotely connected with church growth, while boggling at a $10,000 new outreach actually multiplying congregations. One Church, observing what brings men to Christ, and rejecting such presentation as below its dignity, sticks to its historic methods and misses the shining harvest. Each year numerous opportunities for church growth occur. Many are missed, because churchmen are engaged in "gradualism" or in work designed for other ends than church growth, or because men with a driving concern that others accept Christ are just not there. Many, however, are seized because men, single-eyed to church growth, use methods which multiply churches.

Methods which multiply churches become more and more important in this mid-land. At the left end of the distribution, preparatory methods were necessary. A good case could be made for methods which placated the public or otherwise enabled the mission just to hang on. At the extreme right, methods for large-scale harvesting are clearly in order. But in the middle country—where growth is to be had if it is intelligently and selectively worked for—choice of a suitable method becomes a high duty.

The question is not just "what is good for the existing congregations?" It must be far more definite than that. So many "excellent" activities are possible!

For example, let us imagine a cluster of rural churches made up of poor peasants. About 2,000 communicants are involved. The Church has been growing at about 90 per cent. Shall the world mission send there an agricultural specialist to help raise production?

The question cannot be answered dogmatically. If agricultural instruction accelerates discipling, the answer is clearly yes. If it stops church growth, the answer is clearly no. If it so captures the imagination of the sending Church that great funds are available for *diffuse philanthropy* in the agricultural field, but only small funds for church development, then the answer is probably no. If the agriculturist is concerned with growth and welfare of the churches, at least as much as with technical agricultural procedures and gladly engages in activities which *actually do* maintain church growth, then the answer is probably yes.

Training in how to choose methods which multiply churches in the potentially responsive middle and the aggressively responsive right end of the distribution is highly desirable for all churchmen engaged in mission. As they study the subject, they will find this chapter the beginning of a rewarding experience. To know scores of methods, and the situations in which they have brought about, and can bring about, church growth, is a most valuable part of the equipment of all leaders and missionaries of the Church. They must know their way about on these frontiers.

XVIII

THE CREATION AND SUPPORT OF LEADERSHIP

(1) *Creation of leadership*

In periods of great church growth, one unchanging factor is the creation of leaders. Those heading great church growth rapidly provide leaders one way or another. They seldom lose a church while debating who will lead it, how he will be paid, what his qualifications are to be, and similar questions. They may not be satisfied with the type or quality of leaders they obtain, but within the framework of conditions facing them, they create the best they can. Any leaders are better than none, they say. They believe that the Holy Spirit will raise up prophets, evangelists, and teachers as the Church has need, in a pattern suited to the Church.

Leaders and their families must eat. Consequently, the creation of leaders is intertwined with the creation of systems of support for such leaders. Indeed, so intimate is the relation, that the creation of leaders is at one and the same time the creation of a system of support. If one is done apart from the other, it does not work too well. For example, the Bible School or Theological Seminary might give men fine training only to find that on graduation many take jobs in schools, offices or governmental service. The system of support is as important to the leaders as their educational training—perhaps more so.

Successful multipliers of churches seldom stop inflow while they create leaders and devise systems for their support. This is done during ingathering as an essential part of it. One secret of New Testament growth was that leaders were trained in and by the Church in action. It remains a secret of church growth today. Where the trainees come out of victorious churches, and have been trained by men who are themselves multipliers of the churches, one type of leader is obtained. Where trainees come out of cold churches that have stopped growing, and are trained under academicians, another type results.

(2) *Systems of support*

Six main systems for the support of church leadership can be distinguished. *First*, comes the New Testament system of an unpaid leadership, out of the movement, trained in service. The elders and deacons—the only local leaders of the New Testament churches—earned their living in various secular pursuits. They were encouraged by a small band of sporadically itinerant evangelists who in part supported themselves and in part received offerings from the churches. Thus, new congregations imposed no financial burden whatever on Jerusalem. On the contrary, they were a source of income. The New Testament pattern excels in productivity. None other allows as much flexibility and growth.

Second, the established Churches, through their missions, train and pay preachers and send them to preach to non-Christians and pastor congregations as these arise. This is the most common method in modern times. Thousands of such evangelists are employed all over the world in practically every land. It enables much preaching of the Good News and much pastoring of weak beginning groups in advance of the formation of the indigenous Church. It meets with considerable opposition from some quarters on the ground that it starts churches on the wrong pattern—pastors paid from abroad—but in many places it is difficult to see how the start could be otherwise.

When continued indefinitely it has this disadvantage—that it ties up large resources at places of least return. Where there is least response, and the little churches are weakest numerically and financially, there the parent Church provides fully paid preachers at the rate of one to a few new families; while where men and women in large numbers turn to God, there the world Church hesitates "to pamper" the emergent churches by paying even half the salaries of preachers who look after twenty families and start new churches every year.

Third, pastors or catechists are chosen by the mission from the best of the new converts, given some training, and supported by the land and the new Christians. In many countries of Africa new congregations can be taken in as fast as they come, because the pastor and his wife can grow their food on village-land assigned them. The offerings of the congregations then provide clothes, books and other necessities. The system works as long as pastors are willing to cultivate land. In some places pastors, who are also teachers in the church day school, are excused from compulsory labour by government. The recompense of the pastorate is fourfold—land enough to grow the family food, offerings of the congregations, being excused from road work, and the respect of the community. In such circumstances, few funds from the world Church are involved in starting new congregations.

Fourth, pastors or catechists are supported by school teaching and church offerings with or without mission subsidy. This was the system used in the great expansions of south India. Government paid teachers so much "per pupil who passed an examination." When congregations were first formed from amongst the Malas and Madigas, the missions selected the ablest converts, gave them some training, appointed them as pastor-teachers, and paid them in part out of the government grant received.

At the beginning the congregations seldom gave any large part of their pastor's salary. Yet because of what the pastors earned as teachers, expansion of a large order could take place on comparatively small mission funds. With the passing of the years, greater local contributions made pastors less dependent on government grants; but grants played a crucial part in the initial expansion, without which church growth could not have occurred.

The *fifth* method for providing leaders is for new churches to pay for them entirely. Sometimes new congregations rise as branches of the older ones. The existing laymen and pastors shepherd the branches till they increase sufficiently to call and pay pastors of their own. Sometimes, when they arise at a distance from existing churches, inquirers are asked, "Will you pay and house your teacher-preacher? If so, we can take you now. If not, go back and increase either your individual giving or the numbers of seekers till you can support your pastor." However it may raise funds, the church itself pays the pastor.

The *sixth* method is for the mission to supplement the giving of the local church so that the pastor can be employed. The case constantly arises of a new congregation which must have a pastor of its own in order to flourish but which cannot pay more than a fraction of his salary. The mission pays the balance. The advantage of thus priming the pump is that growth is accelerated. The danger is that, if it starts that way, the local church will let the mission or national Church pay it indefinitely. Where this happens and very few churches go off subsidy, there each new church means new subsidy continued indefinitely. When there are no more foreign funds for new subsidies, church growth grinds to a standstill. This is a common situation.

Various varieties of each of these six systems are found around the world. Number 2 (full mission support) gradually grows into Number 6 (mission subsidy) and that, it is hoped, will grow into Number 5 (full payment by the local churches). Numbers 3 and 4, where pastoral workers draw a large part of their support from the land or teaching or other work, are sometimes so much aided by their assisting missions that they come to resemble Number 6 (mission subsidy). Sometimes they shade off into Number 5 (full payment by the local church).

Each method by which leadership is created and supported is likely to be ardently defended by those operating it. Other systems are rejected out of hand. Churchmen say, "If new congregations, pastored by our system, come in, well and good. Otherwise we cannot take them." Some churchmen for example, turn from the problems of a leadership paid by the mission and espouse wholeheartedly an unpaid leadership. They are likely to say, "We will allow church growth only if it comes with unpaid leaders." Others' main drive is an adequately paid leadership. "Better have no churches," they exclaim, "than these wretched imitations with leaders who are a disgrace to the ministry, so inadequately trained and paid that they attract only the weakest men." Still others, thoroughly convinced that leadership from the beginning must be entirely paid by the local congregations, refuse to develop opportunities for church growth unless those wishing to become Christian are prepared to pay in full their catechist's salary.

The eventual goal is obviously a ministry supported entirely by the local churches. There would be no debate on this point anywhere. Debate rages as to whether complete self-support from the beginning is necessary if the eventual goal is to be reached. Churchmen ask, should churches ever be started with a subsidy to help them support their pastoral workers?

The strength of subsidy is that it enables a start to be made. It is priming the pump. It gives weak beginning groups the advantage of trained full-time leadership. Historically it is the way in which most younger Churches have started. Indeed, many of them started not merely on subsidy but on complete mission support.

The weaknesses of subsidy are several. It is very difficult to terminate. The pastor does not wish to give up his mission subsidy, his one sure source of income, nor does the local church feel able to assume the full burden. Men come to believe that being a Christian involves getting the constant help of a pastor—paid for largely by foreign funds. The subsidy system makes growth dependent on getting further aid from abroad. It blocks great growth. A small increase of some thousands can come in on the subsidy system, but great growth involving scores of thousands can only come on some system whereby each new congregation maintains its own pastor.

Considering these weaknesses, some younger Churches and their assisting missions say, "Churches should never be started with subsidy. It lays the wrong foundation. It gives the wrong impression as to what Christianity really is. It is not *Biblical*. Better to have no new churches start than to have them start on a system which will be a constant handicap."

Considering the values of subsidy, other younger Churches and their assisting missions say, "Under some circumstances, starting with subsidy is necessary. It has been used to God to start many Christward movements, including those younger Churches which now reject it so heartily. We shall use it when necessary. Because weaning is difficult is no reason to start a baby on meat."

In our judgement all six systems have been used of God in varying circumstances to multiply churches. Each has its strengths and weaknesses. It is poor policy to rule that under all circumstances only one is correct. On the contrary, we should use whatever method multiplies the churches, remembering that the best is the one which is self-supporting soonest, and gives the churches a leadership most in harmony with their cultural and economic background.

Churchmen, under whom churches grow, always use the best system they know to create and support leaders; but *they never fail to create leaders* even if they have to use a second, third, or sixth best system of doing it. There is no failure equal to that of coming empty-handed out of a ripe field. Churchmen under whom the churches do not grow, on the other hand, frequently hold on to what they consider an ideal system for creating and supporting leaders and refuse growth when it does not come in that groove.

(3) *The standard of the ministry*

The standard of the ministry and the training which produces it have a pronounced bearing on church-growth. The standard involves the degree of training and the amount of salary—in relation to the cultural and economic level of the members.

Growth can start vigorously only when leaders who fit new churches are made available as fast as new churches can be established. The catechists or pastors must be in tune with their people, must like them, and feel at home with them. Their degree of education must not be so small that they cannot serve their people, nor so great that they look down on them from superior heights. Ideally they should be of the same social stratum as the members and educated somewhat but not too far above it.

Church-growth can continue vigorous only when funds to support these new workers are—one way or another—made available as rapidly as new churches can be established. Ideally, this means leaders of such a standard of salary that the new churches can—and will—pay them. There is no surer way to choke church growth than to create a highly educated one-level ministry which by training is out of tune with the rank and file of new members and will not work for what the new churches will pay.

Let us take a case showing how disregard of this factor can arrest church-growth. Each of the five old line boards in Puerto Rico has a younger Church of from 4,000 to 7,000 communicants. Candidates for the ministry in these churches are given training in the Union Theological Seminary at Rio Piedras and then go out to pastorates where—with the exception of the large city and suburban churches—the local church-giving is supplemented by the boards, so that the ministers may receive adequate recompense. One Church ruled that all its ministers must receive $200 a month. Since new congregations seldom can pay this, expansion involves subsidy and costs the supporting boards, say, $1,000 a year per congregation. No wonder that in one younger Church no new congregations have been started for over fifteen years.

Shall we conclude that church expansion is financially impossible in Puerto Rico? It would be easy to do so, except for the fact that the churches of the Assemblies of God are growing rapidly there. Their standard of the ministry is a spiritual standard, not educational or cultural; and their standard of recompense is what each congregation chooses to pay. Their leaders come right out of the churches. Some are part-time, some full-time, some voluntary, some men of little education and paid poorly, some men of superior education and paid handsomely. Their top leaders are men of marked ability. Thus, while the Assemblies of God maintain their pastors, they are not bound by any system of pay; and while they expect their ministers to be men of God and know the Bible, they do not necessarily equate this with a college education. Their rapid growth may be due more to their method of creating and supporting their ministry than to their much discussed fervency.

The standard of the ministry today is usually viewed from a totally different angle—that of fitting it for the burdens of top administration, heretofore carried by missionaries. From this angle, the welfare of the younger Churches lies in developing highly trained ministers and getting the existing churches to support them. The Church needs a highly trained ministry—that is part of the picture; but it is not the whole picture. Such a ministry cannot meet the challenge of growth.

Highly paid and trained ministers are several stages removed from the common people. Starting new churches with such ministers usually involves subsidy, wholly apart from the problem of getting them in sufficient numbers for existing churches and administrative positions. Under subsidy, growth continues as far as foreign funds will allow and then stops. Eschewing subsidy, however, does not solve the problem. The highly trained and paid are still several stages removed from the common people, and it is very difficult to get churches to employ them, and to persuade them to serve for what they will receive. The amount and nature of church-growth is, indeed, significantly influenced by the standards of the ministry required, by any system, for the creation and support of leaders.

(4) *Three kinds of leaders*

Growing churches require three varieties of leaders. Methods which produce such favour church-growth. Concentration on a single variety discourages it.

Outside of a few advanced democratic countries, society is divided into the classes and the masses. In even such an advanced land as the Philippines, for example, the income of the professional managerial class averages about 2,000 pesos a year, while that of the fisherman, peasant, and landless labourer, averages about 400 pesos. In the former, high school and college education is the rule; while in the latter, the completion of four or five grades of schooling would be the average. In many lands the gap is even more pronounced.

Urban churches around mission stations are likely to be made up of a fair cross-section of the middle, lower, and labouring classes. But whenever the churches multiply greatly, congregations of the classes and the congregations of the masses come into being. The former have one standard of education and income, the latter have another. Two levels of leaders are needed: one for the congregations where the average annual income of the members is "2,000 pesos," and one for those where the average income is "400."

If church-growth is expected from among the classes, then pastors are required whose standard of education and salary fit that kind of congregation. If church-growth is expected from among the masses, then pastors are required whom the new churches of the common man can support and to whom pastoring the masses is an agreeable task. Administrators, carrying the responsibility for the guidance of the churches, should estimate in what proportion growth will come from the classes and the masses and prepare suitable numbers of paid leaders on each level.

The third variety of leader is the unpaid layman. Deacons and elders, teachers and youth workers, secretaries and treasurers, board members and choir singers—all are vital to the life of the church. This is a truism in America. Lay leadership, however, can be easily overlooked in a congregation fresh from paganism.

Training the paid leaders—the village pastors or catechists—is such a large task, and training a raw and often illiterate laity involves such difficulties, that lay training is often neglected.

Lay leadership is tremendously important for church growth. When churches start spreading in New Testament fashion across the country, laymen are frequently the agents of extension. Furthermore, as foreign aid and mission subsidies come to play a smaller part in the younger Churches, the importance of unpaid lay leaders increases. "How to train laymen to proclaim an evangel which converts" should be part of the curriculum in all pastoral, ministerial, and missionary training. The creation, in every new field, of a great body of Christian youth and adults who know why they are Christians, and who can convince others that the Christian faith should be accepted, is essential to church-growth. Methods which do this are needed.

(5) *Institutions for training leaders*

Let us now turn to the institutions for creating leaders. Our first example will show how the kind of training given bears on church multiplication and self-support.

The rapidly growing Anglican Church in Ruanda numbers about 100,000 people. It creates and supports its leaders in the following fashion. It has hundreds of village congregations—some big, some small. For its paid leaders, it seeks the best young men out of these village congregations. Up to the present time most of them have very little formal education. Some of them are not much more than literate when they first become church workers.

The first appointment is to be an assistant in a small congregation. The worker gets free land from the village for cultivation. He —or more likely his wife—raises all his own food. He gets little besides. If he appears promising material, he is sent for a few month's instruction to his station school. If he passes, he gets his first Station Letter and goes back to a slightly larger responsibility. If he makes good, in a year or two he comes back for a second few months in the station school where he gets still further reading, writing, arithmetic, elementary Bible, and churchmanship.

After he has served six or eight years and obtained his fourth Station Letter, he may be assigned to the supervision of eight or ten village churches. Making good here requires administrative ability. He will continue to farm village land for his food and receive contributions of cash and kind. There are scores of such supervising pastors, each tested for years in the service and found devout, loyal, and able.

From these men the best are selected annually to go to the Warner Memorial College for a three-year course. While there they raise their own family food on the college fields and after passing the courses are ordained as fully qualified clergymen of the Church of England. The Church has secured for itself an élite corps of tested, trained clergymen, few if any of whom are even grade school graduates, whom the churches can support, and who are content with the recompense they receive.

They do not desert the pastorate to go to highly paid commercial and government jobs. They are sympathetic to the system which produced them and are prepared to use it for the indefinite expansion of the Church. It provides abundant men who fit the incoming congregations. Systematic selection also provides top level leaders.

The Ruanda Scheme illustrates well that training is not for the sake of some abstract standard but for the sake of the growth and welfare of the Church. Ministers need training which enables them to make churches grow and take in the multitudes awaiting salvation. Wherever great surging growth occurs, there something like the Ruanda Scheme should prove profitable.

However, for ordinary situations, the main means of training leaders must remain the Theological Seminary and the Bible School, or Theological Training School as it is called in South-East Asia. In these important institutions young men, just through their secular schooling, are given several years' training and emerge as catechists, village pastors, and ministers.

What kind of theological training; what kind of curriculum; what kind of teacher turns out men under whom sound and maximum church growth takes place? Is it the teacher whose study of current church history has taught him the structure of church-growth and how to get it in his particular land? Is it the teacher who recognizes, welcomes, and knows how to develop people movements to Christ?

Nowhere can the "cultural overhang" more greatly damage a younger Church than in theological training. A seminary which takes its curriculum and its standards from the famous seminaries of the West is in grave danger. It forgets that to the Churches of the West great numerical increase is neither necessary for survival nor possible. The Evangelical Churches of America, for example, could not treble in the next decade. There is not that number of unchurched people left in America. But most Evangelical Churches in the non-Occident could treble their membership and still have less than 5 per cent of the total population. Indeed, they must more than treble if they are to fulfil their calling. Some of them must grow greatly merely to survive. Hence we should discover and include in the curricula of the younger seminaries subjects that will help students to multiply the churches they serve.

(6) *While harvest proceeds*

We are not called on to create a static ministry for static Churches content to remain at their present size in the midst of millions of the winnable. We are called to create a ministry which will keep growing Churches growing and start non-growing Churches on the road of great growth.

Training carried on during ingathering, as a part of the process, produces leaders who know how to make churches multiply. The students and the staff have come out of growing churches. They themselves may be converts. They are immersed in a victorious forward movement. As they study New Testament, Old Testament, Homiletics, and Theology, they are focused on church growth. Student preachers "bring in" new congregations or hear about their fellow students who have done so. The whole atmosphere of the institution living in the midst of growth is different from that where the students are of non-growing churches and the teachers are concerned about various other aspects of the Christian life divorced from conversion and church multiplication.

What happens when the existing Church has come to a standstill? The answer lies, in part, in a seminary staff which itself marches under the Great Commission, regards winning men to Christ as ten times more important than anything else it does, holds a "Pauline" or "temporal-eternal" philosophy of mission, seeks to find out how church-growth can occur today in its land, and transmits these convictions and this knowledge to its students. In part, the answer lies in the creation and support of leaders who fit *new* congregations. Such leaders should be turned out as fast as new congregations can be gathered, at the point where they are being won, from among the men and women who compose them.

XIX

CHECKING METHODS AGAINST ACTUAL GROWTH

In most forms of human endeavour progress is accelerated by constantly checking performance against defined goals. The navigator repeatedly brings the ship back on course. The teacher gives examinations to find how well lessons have been learned. The business firm measures sales in various territories to discover favourable markets, able men, and successful selling methods. It would seem natural for those carrying out the Great Commission to check achievements in church-growth to find how well they are getting on with making disciples of all nations.

Yet this is seldom done. Instead we have a plethora of schemes which "ought to be good" for the world mission. For example, an American professor, after returning from a study tour among the younger Churches in India was speaking earnestly at a missionary conference in London. "We must make the churches less barren and more beautiful in the Indian mode," he said. "Only then can we hold Indian youth. The missionary must never impose his ideas on younger Churches. By use of cultural styles congenial to the people being evangelized, the Gospel must be made intelligent to them. A Christian home marked by full respect for personality in the family circle is essential to the growth of the Church. The Church must become involved in all of life. Conversations with non-Christian religions must go forward on every level. The whole basis of financial relationship must be changed so that the self-respect of our sister Churches be not infringed."

My fellow professor's remarks are typical. Gatherings of churchmen to consider missions seldom fail today to stress these and similar items. *A priori* solutions are poured forth in great profusion. In the context of the speech they sound plausible. To single them out for criticism or refutation would be ungracious. They represent theories, strategies, and hobbies of earnest men and women. They reflect some thought, bias, or special interest of the propounder rather than any measured welfare of the churches. Yet they are set forth as if they were the last word in statesmanship among younger Churches—all younger Churches!

Some of these suggestions under some circumstances may be desirable for some churches. The difficulty, however, is that this mass of *a priori* solutions to secondary problems comes to be regarded as "missions today." They are projected in such volume that they obscure the central irreplaceable essence of mission. In emphasizing their own specialties which "ought to work" and "ought to be good for the younger Churches," they so diminish the importance of the actual propagation of churches that any attempt to measure it seems fatuous. Seminaries teach missionary methods—but seldom measure the degree to which their graduates multiply churches. Church statistics, of course, are reported from every field, but seldom used except when strikingly favourable. Actual church growth is rarely carefully checked.

A book on Japan states: "Extensive programmes of newspaper evangelism, advertising, correspondence courses, monthly publications, visitation, loan libraries, and Christian book stores are being used to lead to Christ the people who are scattered across the land." But we must ask, "Do they in fact lead to Christ? Or are they being used in hope that they will? And is there a check to see what is actually accomplished?"

The thought of measuring the value of an enterprise by the number of its members is widely repugnant. Since it would go hard with those working in irresponsive fields, they vigorously oppose it. Since the situation facing younger Churches is so extremely varied, all fear a uniform test. Even those in places of great growth, and subject to the Protestant "mind-blocks" described in Chapter 3, are often fatigued and sigh, "If only our predecessors had not allowed such growth. For heaven's sake, do not test mission against church growth." Such is the hostile climate which any proposal to test methods against church growth encounters.

Yet, without testing, we stand in the midst of unlimited confusion. As the conscientious churchman regards the many factors connected with church-growth, and the many popular aims and methods having little to do with it, he becomes confused. As he sees how easily the steady progress of churches can be upset and movements to Christ die, and how often secondary considerations determine outcomes, he becomes more confused. As long as the definition of the chief end varies, and he depends on *a priori* judgements as to what ought to work, his confusion will increase. In the presence of many "equally good" theories of missions, many "equally desirable" outcomes, and many "equally wise" churchmen, all that any Christian can do is to let the process of "missions" churn on as it will, and to fit in his own labours wherever the swirling tides and changing currents place him. He will be more comfortable if he can convince himself that God has placed him there.

In the presence of winnable multitudes, however, and contemplating vast meadows from which the ice sheet has retreated, is any such standardless outpouring of labour God's plan? Is it even necessary?

"Parallelism," referred to earlier, necessarily results from absence of measurement. One man's opinion is as good as his brother's. Hence every piece of mission work which can once get recognized is as good as any other piece. For example, a mission board set out to judge the value of its labours around the world. All concerned contributed their opinions as to what constituted "good missions," thus building up a criterion of judgement which represented not primarily the Church and its welfare, but every existing enterprise. The result was that, after enormous amounts of time and money had been spent evaluating the far flung work according to these all-inclusive criteria, every enterprise carried on by the board had been abundantly justified!

On the other hand, there are those whose main criterion is *the degree of church growth obtained.* The value of every method and every piece of work is estimated after measuring the actual church-growth obtained from it. When churchmen following this method inquire whether method D is good, bad, or indifferent, they are not limited to balancing the opinions of X against those of Y, having previously decided that X and Y are equally wise. They have measured, and know how much church growth method D has produced. An objective factor is introduced. It is, to be sure, not the only factor; but it is one chief factor. No longer are they limited by what someone thinks ought to happen. They have found out what has happened.

In responsive populations, where men are being discipled by some branch of the Church of Christ, correct phrases, impeccable resolutions, or even deeply Christian longings, are not enough. There, Christian Mission which fails to establish church after church, fails. It is good to *say*, "All of life must be claimed for Christ," "We must show Christ's victory over the gulfs which separate men," "We are called to relate our faith to the problems of the industrial age." It is nearer the target to *say*, "We must not only present the Gospel to the industrial masses, but must also bring them into the Church." But where churches can be established, the Christian Mission succeeds not by correct sayings and good intentions but by actually establishing groups of believers—who can be counted. Hence, we advocate careful intelligent measurement of the actual degree of church-growth obtained.

Churchmen should, however, apply this criterion of church-growth with spiritual sensitivity. It cannot be done mechanically as if Christians were cars rolling off assembly lines. The spread of the Gospel is qualitatively different from the production of things. Imponderables are involved. Persons are concerned. The motive is compassion not competition. The process itself is not one where men use others for their own convenience; but one which brings together God's love, man's labour, and man's penitence and obedience, and all this for the sake of those accepting Christ.

Estimation of results is a reasonable Christian procedure and must be made. It is also a delicate one. It involves spiritual values which cannot be counted, as well as Christians who can be. Simply counting heads, for example, is not sufficient; neither is simply not counting them. Paul's epistles have a value far beyond the numbers of Christians and churches he brought into existence; yet they would neither have been written nor transmitted if his labours had not produced countable Christians and countable churches. Some say that men cannot produce Christians at all (that is done by the Holy Spirit); yet our Lord plainly commands us to "make disciples." He also spoke of winning disciples as if it were a production operation, cutting and carrying in sheaves. And, in His parable, the number of talents the servants brought to their Lord had a crucial significance.

Qualify and understand it as we may, to check our aims against our achievement is most necessary. The mission field has great opportunity for scattered effort. Human needs are multitudinous. There are so many good things to do. Were there unlimited resources, so that all the hungry could be fed, all the naked clothed, all the illiterates taught, and all the winnable won, the case would be radically different. Today these tasks are attempted with limited resources. The Churches are constantly faced, not with situations which can be fully met by doing both, but with those which can only be partially met by doing one or the other. *Which are to be left undone?* This question should stand squarely in the centre of Church thinking today in regard to its world mission. Every churchman has to leave some things undone. Which should they be? There is no escaping this question. A decision to undertake one enterprise means leaving others crying for action. Hence intelligent decision requires both a clear cut theory of mission which states the priorities; and constant measurement of achievements so that the theory believed to be God's will—and not some other which creeps in the back door—may be implemented.

Checking against church-growth is needed because so many mission enterprises are inevitably and properly launched in hope. Failing constant and accurate check, exploratory moves which did not pan out are carried forward for decades. Enterprises, established that the Church might grow, continue to receive support for generations after it has become clear that through them the Church is not growing. These resources are then not available for populations where the Church can grow.

Checking against church-growth is much more needed by missions than by self-supporting local churches. If some theory of what is good for the local church is put into operation by its minister and does not prove beneficial, either that theory is jettisoned or the minister is. Local churches have a built-in check. But in missions, since the supporters are not at hand and cannot know the field, a theory once put into operation can continue for years, indeed for decades, without check. Once church-growth has been discarded as a chief (but not the only) factor in evaluation, there is no way to judge whether a given enterprise is good or not. "Of course, it is good. It has to be good, whatever it be." It would be a poor enterprise, indeed, if, with the salary of several missionaries and an annual budget of thousands, it could not justify itself as a fine Christian undertaking!

What part of "cultural overhang" should the churchman renounce? He is well aware of its danger. Yet in the absence of measurement which determines how well the objective of church multiplication is being reached, a churchman in Indonesia might well wonder whether avoiding "cultural overhang" means wearing Indonesian clothes, committing to notation Indonesian tunes and writing hymns to fit them, or rethinking his theology to make it more Indonesian? It is worth while studying all this in order to see what prevents the Church from expanding and remove the obstacle. When we test every method against "what multiplies the Churches" we shall be able to abandon the most damaging of the "cultural overhangs."

How about the unripe fields? Where the Church cannot grow, we find many projects which should work, but don't—schools which should produce a generation of men open to the Gospel, but don't; hospitals whose many works of mercy should convince men of the beneficent intent of Christians, but don't; and evangelism which should plant churches, but doesn't. These are continued for the very good reason that nothing seems more likely to work. As between A, B and C none of which produce church-growth, it is immaterial which we use. In such fields it is well not to test, lest we become discouraged. In these fields the practical question is not "what can we do to make the Church grow" but "what can we do to keep Christian activity of any sort alive." Hence entirely unripe fields should not check all activities against church-growth.

How about institutions? Here is a school full of Christian youth, a college for the intelligentsia of the world, a public health enterprise for people of the world, none of whom are likely to become Christian, a theological seminary training the ministry for several small non-growing Churches and one large growing one, a mission hospital which can provide fine medical care for a small Christian community because it also serves a large non-Christian community. Are all these to be measured against church-growth?

There are three varieties of institutions. Each requires a different answer.

First, there are the institutions in advance of the Church—Christian hospitals in Arabia, Christian schools in Benares and other strongholds of Hinduism. Even evangelism carried on with a professional staff where very few if any become Christian becomes a kind of institution. The task of these enterprises is to stay alive, bearing as much witness to Christ as possible. It would be foolish to apply the criterion of church-growth to them. They are successful if they just keep going. However, in view of the ever-increasing response to the Gospel, the number of such institutions grows less every passing year.

Second, there are institutions dominating a non-growing Church. We think of the institutions in connection with younger Church Z of Chipania which had a membership of 4,890 in 1924 and 4,986 in 1954. It is now served by two hospitals, eighteen grade schools or parts of them, four high schools, one college, and one theological seminary. These absorb 92 per cent of the missionary assistance given to the Church, and 78 per cent of the budget. They render wonderful service to at least the urban members of the Church. Through their intimate connection with the Christian community of about 10,000 souls, the witness they bear is indubitably Christian. They are the manifestation of Christianity which the world sees. In the Christian community the choice positions and appointments are those in the institutions, which offer financial security and social acceptance. The majority of the staff are church leaders. This, with variations, is a common picture of the institutions connected with younger Churches. Thousands of missionaries and other churchmen are immersed in institutions which dominate a non-growing Church. In what sense and in what way shall we check all activities here against church-growth?

At first glance it may appear entirely impractical. The hospital is a hospital, we say, not a conversion agency. It is concerned with giving men physical health. The school is a school, not a conversion agency. It is concerned with giving good education. It would be unfitting—and perhaps un-Christian—to measure these institutions against church-growth. This is the answer of a few Christians. It is the answer which many people of the world would like to hear from all mission institutions. Some governments pass laws requiring this answer. But, if this be our answer, we must face two consequences: (*a*) our mission then settles down contentedly to spending 92 per cent of our missionary assistance and 78 per cent of our cash assistance in philanthropic enterprises; and about 15 per cent of its resources in a fruitless effort to carry out the Great Commission; (*b*) the 85 per cent spent in this irresponsive field for philanthropy will not be available for church multiplication in ripened fields. Ripened harvests will rot in the fields while the world mission of the Church maintains hospitals and schools for people who reject the Good News.

The first glance, however, is faulty. It errs in concluding that where a Church of 4,986 has been created, there church-growth is impossible. It errs in assuming a homogeneous population, all of it equally indifferent. It errs in not discerning ripened and ripening populations in the 20,000 square miles across which the existing churches are spread. It errs in accepting the smooth suggestion of Satan that there is something immoral and un-Christian in Christian doctors and school men unashamedly and openly urging all men, their patients, pupils, and others, to accept Jesus Christ as Saviour. It errs in hinting that the criterion of church-growth had better be altered lest opposition arise.

A second glance shows that constantly measuring the effectiveness for church-growth of all activities is both feasible and necessary. Are all Christians who pass through these institutions, observing that the leading staff members live to share Christ with others, made alive to church-growth; or, observing something else are they deadened to it? Are the churchmen, who earn their living as teachers or physicians, fervent Christians—teaching branch Sunday Schools, attending cottage prayer meetings, writing tracts commending Christ to their fellow citizens, preaching in chapel and in public, reading the Bible and singing God's praises, both before their pupils and patients and in public places so that they are known as desiring that all men should become disciples of Christ? The non-growing church-mission organism (congregations and their dominating institutions) also, in fact, continually looks out on ripening fields—and would find them if it sought them. If it were more accustomed to checking all its activities against church growth, it would be more likely to welcome ripening fields and send suitable harvesting teams into them.

The institutions dominating a non-growing Church should regularly check their activities against church-growth. Only as church-growth is measured and known can institutions help their churches take advantage of fruitful situations. The more influential the institutions, *vis-à-vis* the churches, the more important does it become that they be earnestly working for church-growth.

Third, there are institutions serving a growing Church. Here the institution is justified by its growing churches. The schools of a flourishing Church to which come boys from 100 congregations are essential parts of the growth process. So are the hospitals and other auxiliary institutions. Those exposed to their influence go out into ripe populations. It becomes more necessary than ever to measure such institutions against church-growth. For *them* to have little or no connection with church-growth is tragic. A high school in Ghana, let us say, where every graduate is likely to be a Christian going out into tremendously open and ripe fields, should constantly measure itself against church-growth. Do its students in fact go out afire to increase the Church? Are its teachers exemplary laymen in that they are working at church multiplication in the surrounding countryside? Are its Bible courses and worship services aglow with consciousness of the uniquely favourable opportunity for church-growth in the Colony, Ashanti, and the Northern Territories? Does it have student organizations out of which come both abundant volunteers for evangelism in the neighbourhood of the school and a great band of paid and unpaid missionaries of the Cross, spending their vacations evangelizing in the *zongoes* and Northern Territories? Does the school function as the "Brains" of the expanding Church—or is it a training ground for government clerks?

It is in these ways that institutions serving growing Churches check their activities against the growth of the Church. They should not relax in the knowledge that they are institutions of a growing Church. They should devise measurements which test the many ways in which they also can play an honourable part in victory.

Who checks against church-growth?

The most fruitful check is that self-check carried out by every churchman. There was the national who came at the age of thirty-two to the position of head teacher in a central school. One day, as he ran through his files, he realized that while he had been the means under God of leading some students to Christ, an organization of ex-students might lead many more. His first attempt met with failure. Later efforts, corrected in various ways, met with success. God thus used a head-master to establish churches and bring to many the inestimable benefits of faith in Christ. The total resources available to the World Church in the lives of its church leaders are tremendous beyond computation. But the only persons who can check these lives are the churchmen themselves.

Local congregations also and mission stations have a very wide sphere of labour in which, without referring to anyone outside their own circle, they can survey their activities against the opportunities to multiply churches and can then take appropriate steps. The local church in Japan, seeing the transformation wrought by *Homon Dendo* (organized visitation evangelism) in other congregations, will start the same kind of thing itself if its aim is church-growth. Churchmen in mission station M, where membership has declined in the past twenty-three years from 7,400 to 4,200, will search their hearts and check whether all their activities are resulting in church-growth.

Missions and Churches are the units where action is most necessary. They are very nearly the "final authority." A heavy responsibility rests on them. It will be painful for some to dig up membership records and measure their scores of activities against actual church-growth; but it will be a rewarding undertaking. They might draft and send to each of their churchmen the following enquiry:

> What part in the growth of the churches is played by the piece of work for which you have responsibility? Is it adequate? Have you recently been responsible for the establishment of any congregation? Or the conversion of any person? What more could you do? Would you welcome a joint effort to multiply your effectiveness for church growth and pledge yourself to increased effort both through your congregation and in other ways? Your congregation has grown 23 per cent in the last decade, but all of this is due to Christians from other places settling in your town. How can *you* win more from the world? Other churches are doing it, can yours?

Suppose all church and mission work were to be painstakingly surveyed from this point of view and the per cent of increase of each congregation be correctly estimated, prominently displayed, and discussed at annual meetings. Suppose that all meetings of executive committees were to devote only three-quarters of their time to discussing purchase of property, transfer of workers, building of budgets, repair of buildings, law-suits, and other routine matters, and one-quarter to discussing increase of membership—how much had been accomplished and how to accomplish more. The shock to some executive committees would be devastating. At first they would scarcely know how to fill the four or five hours thus provided. Still they would gradually become accustomed to the new order and would find it yielding rich returns.

Lastly, the boards and contributing congregations of the older Churches should cultivate the habit of checking their world-wide activities by the resulting growth of Churches. One of the most rapidly growing younger Churches presents, to its Division of World Mission, percentages of church-growth achieved by every one of its church units. Thus the Division in its decisions can take account of the vital factor of church-growth.

Individuals, congregations, Churches and Missions, boards and older Churches, all in their own spheres need to cultivate the habit of measuring "church-growth achieved" and regarding it as one of the most significant factors in the world mission. Only then can they rightly estimate the value of theories of mission, forms of organization, and methods of operation. Measurement is not easy. It cannot occur automatically. Yet it must be done if the younger Churches are to enter their heritage and the world mission is to fulfil its high calling. The effort required will be abundantly rewarded.

PART V

ORGANIZATION IN CHURCH-GROWTH

XX

EXPANSION AHEAD OF THE CHURCH

(I) The Christian Church in Antioch arose months before Jerusalem knew about it. When "the report concerning them came to the ears of the church which was in Jerusalem, they sent forth Barnabas to Antioch."

When Paul, passing through the upper country in the year 52, came to Ephesus he found there about a dozen disciples. They did not know of baptism in Christ's name or of the Holy Spirit. Yet they considered themselves disciples of the Messiah and were so considered by Paul and Luke.

The Christian church in Rome arose before Paul arrived there. When Paul first came to Rome, he stayed for seven days with a band of Christians in Puteoli, about a hundred miles from Rome. When he reached Rome he found a church (Acts 28: 15 and Romans 16: 5) meeting in the house of Priscilla and Aquila. In view of Puteoli, there may have been several churches in and near the imperial city.

We can be sure that these recorded instances are but a small fraction of the total number of churches which sprang up ahead of any formal teaching, authorized visitation, or connection with the existing churches. There seems no reason to doubt the tradition in the Church of Ethiopia that Candace's Treasurer, a Jew by birth or conversion, after his brief instruction and his baptism by Philip, not only "went on his way rejoicing," but formed a band of Christians at the Ethiopian capital. These read the book of Isaiah (and other Old Testament books?) and, rejoicing that the promised

Messiah had come, became disciples of Christ. Doubtless many churches arose on very scanty instruction and understanding.

The New Testament, while pointing out that the understanding of Christ was only partial in these bands of believers resulting from expansion ahead of the Church, nevertheless counts them as Christians. In Rome the band is called a "church." In Ephesus the dozen men are called "disciples"—which word Luke invariably uses for disciples of Christ. Luke calls those in Puteoli "some of the brotherhood," and of those in Antioch he affirms that before Barnabas' arrival they had "turned to the Lord," were "faithful to the Lord," and had received "the grace of God."

It is not necessary to assume that "the church" was formed in completeness when the first band in each place first believed, before the arrival of any apostle. Free churchmen will hold one opinion on that matter and Anglicans another. All that we are concerned to underline is that the New Testament mode of expansion included, as a major factor, the establishment of bands of worshippers in advance of formal teaching of doctrine, authorized visitation, or official connection with the Church at Jerusalem. Some of these bands were heretical from the point of view of the Jerusalem Church. But, as the elders at Jerusalem regarded them, they must have remembered and quoted the words of our Lord recorded in Mark 9: 38–41. At any rate, guided by the Holy Spirit, they claimed them all as brethren, disciples, churches, and fellow Christians. It is not without significance that the disciples were first called Christians in a rather irregular church, whose tremendous new departure precipitated many battles and much heartache in the already established churches of Christ.

(II) Many students of younger Churches and Missions consider church-growth exclusively in terms of an orderly induction of believers into correct church patterns. Their own, of course. The degree to which ardent Christians think of church expansion in terms of their particular patterns is amazing. They will have no hand in a pattern of organization, ministerial training and support, or worship, different from their own. They will even reject ingathering according to their own previous pattern. I once read aloud to a churchman an account of a great ingathering which occurred 100 years ago in his own Church. In a tremendous experience men and women "poured out their souls in agonizing prayer and uncontrolled weeping" and on conversion were "filled with joy unspeakable." "Thank God," he ejaculated, "we do not permit that sort of thing any more." "Whether the churches grow or not?" I asked. "Whether the churches grow or not," he replied emphatically.

The world mission of the church at myriad points invites men to become Christians but always according to some exactly defined and rigid ecclesiastical pattern. Presbyterian churchmen lead their converts into patterns congenial to them. Similarly, Episcopalians, Disciples, Assemblies of God, and every other Church baptize men into their specific moulds. Since each existing Church has a long history in which its pattern has been defined and defended, the convert comes into a predetermined organization, form of worship, and statement of doctrine. The ecumenical outlook today assists in increasing the toleration with which other patterns are viewed, but so far it has not notably increased willingness to search out more effective patterns and use them. Lutherans in Puerto Rico follow their own distinctive pattern, which has achieved inconsiderable growth, rather than switch to a Baptist pattern which has produced great church-growth. Both eschew the Assembly of God pattern which has produced much more growth than either. Evangelistic missions stick to evangelistic paths even when those are not as successful as educational paths, and *vice versa*.

(III) It is against this background that we must view a very widespread phenomenon—the rise of independent younger Churches. One does not travel far among Chinese before meeting True Jesus and Little Flock churches. These indigenous Chinese churches have arisen outside the orbit of western effort. No one knows their number or extent. With a simple New Testament organization, a high degree of biblical faith and great local autonomy, they spring up in widely separated places.

In Japan there is an interesting Christian movement. After a term in Japan as a missionary, Emil Bruner, the famous theologian, feels that the assemblies of this movement, arising outside the orbit of the regular Churches, are very like New Testament congregations.

In India, Bakht Singh is a prophet of power. Bible in hand, he preaches in English or Hindi, to large crowds for two or three hours at a stretch. He has been greatly used of God to revive nominal Christians. He is a strong independent character of extreme dedication. He affiliates with no mission or younger Church. He arouses the most varied responses among churchmen—some revere him and annually call him for meetings to revive the spiritual life. Others oppose him furiously as a divisive element. In some places where he repeatedly speaks he founds no separate church. In other places churches arise which regard him as their spiritual guide. He has formed these recently into an independent younger Church.

In Africa hundreds of independent Churches have arisen—most of them with a few congregations, some of them with a large number. Geoffrey Parrinder, one of the professors at Ibadan University in Nigeria, says that contrary to common belief many of these African Churches are intensely and literally biblical. A few have incorporated elements of animism, sanctioned polygamy, and do not regard Christ and the Scriptures as final authority. But most of them are clearly Christian and rather orthodox. They multiply and reach into new communities on an entirely self-supporting and indigenous basis.

In the Philippines the *Iglesia Ni Christo* has at least 200,000 members. It has built several million-dollar churches in Manila and Baguio. It has many doctors, lawyers, teachers, government servants and other such people on its rolls, in addition to large numbers of humbler members of society. Its highly disciplined services of worship would be creditable to any Church in any land. It receives not a penny of subsidy or foreign assistance, nor does it have any foreign missionary helpers. It started in 1914 and represents a colossal indigenous growth. Its degrees of dedication, knowledge of the Scriptures, and stewardship are high. It holds that it is the only valid Church, but so do all Roman Catholics and many Episcopalians. It is governed autocratically by its leader, Felix Manalo, but so was the Church in Geneva by its leader, John Calvin.

All these Churches, and some others, have arisen independent of direct Western effort in the new climate of receptivity. Like the New Testament churches, they have made some "new departures." Brother Felix Manalo teaches that he himself is the angel and the

Philippines are the "land of the rising sun" described in Revelation 7: 2. The congregations which seem to Dr. Bruner so like New Testament churches call themselves a "No-Church" movement. Some of the African Churches have dancing as a part of the communion service. Yet they all believe themselves to be genuine Christian Churches. And they reach out to regions untouched by the West, as well as to nominal Christians.

(IV) For two hours people poured into the great Rizal stadium in Manila. They arrived on foot, by car, in buses, and on cycles. They filled the grandstand and the great circle of seats around the field. Then the chains were opened and they flooded out into the field in front of the stand on which Billy Graham was to speak. From a massed choir of 1,000 voices, swelling harmony reverberated across the stillness of the night in praise to God. Scripture was read. Dr. Graham spoke for an hour and then invited men and women to accept Christ: 5,000 filed from their seats to stand in a huge circle around the evangelist. Some were Christian young people who had never yielded to Christ. A sizeable number were men and women of the world whom God had touched that night. They filled in cards. Workers gathered these up. After prayer, the meeting ended and those who had accepted Christ scattered all over Manila and the central part of the Philippines.

In Delhi, 12,000 people each night, many of them men and women of the world, poured into a huge shimmering *shamiana* to hear Dr. Graham. In South India, over 100,000 gathered at one place. In Bombay tremendous crowds assembled. Everywhere large numbers from both the Church and the world "decided for Christ." They filled in cards and scattered to their homes.

In Japan, at meetings led by Dr. Stanley Jones and Dr. Kagawa, those who signed cards saying that they wanted to be Christians numbered over 100,000 and over 280,000 respectively.

Whether those who accepted Christ went on to become practising Christians depended on how they were followed up. Dr. Graham, Dr. Kagawa and Dr. Jones ceaselessly stress this point. There is much to indicate that the number from the world who accepted Christ was much greater than the number who became baptized practising Christians.

In many lands correspondence courses in the Bible are now proving popular. Scores of thousands in a little country like Formosa enrol for a Bible study course of eight lessons. Radio programmes help to swell the number of inquirers and participants. Each receives a Gospel and begins a series of lessons designed to present the Christian Way. Many who take the course start going to church. Some become disciples of Christ. There is also a startling response to correspondence courses in Japan, the Philippines, Formosa, Ceylon, India, and other countries.

The efforts described above are intended to lead converts into the established Churches under whose auspices their work is carried on. Bible correspondents are encouraged to get into touch with the nearest church. Those who accept Christ in public meetings are helped to fill in cards and a great effort is made to contact them later and bring them into an existing Church. All this is excellent.

Yet it does not seem to result in great accessions to the existing churches. Is this because the decisions are superficial? Some think so. Or is it that the new media of communication reach units of society which are socially, religiously, and sometimes geographically distant from the established congregations. Is the Gospel bound by the particular problems of the modern missionary movement and the modern younger Churches? For example, as upper caste Hindus in Bombay and Delhi look at the existing Christian Churches, they see them as clubs of beef-eaters who, up till recently, were quite largely guided by white men, and whose ways of worship are still distinctly un-Indian. Becoming Christian means separating from all previous ties and going into these churches. Being baptized means becoming parts of these strange communities. There is resistance at just that point.

One additional method of extension by the existing Churches, through their great meetings and their new media of communications, might be to invite respondents to secure New Testaments and form worshipping-groups of their own folk, assuring them that all who accept Jesus Christ as sole Lord and Saviour, and the Scriptures as the rule of faith and practice, who assemble for Bible study, prayer, and praise, and live their lives under His hand, *are* disciples of Christ, do receive the Holy Spirit, and *are* saved. In addition to the invitation to seek out a nearby church, an alternate suggestion might be made that a group of like-minded people might assemble, and, in whatever way seemed best to them (Japanese, Chinese, Indian, or African) to worship God-in-Christ, seek His will as revealed in the New Testament, and live according to it. Correspondence-courses might make this method an optional choice and mail biblical instructions—to be verified from the Word—to all who asked for them, telling them how to organize worshipping groups of indigenous Christians.

In some parts of Latin America something of this sort is now going on, and little churches, with hardly any connection with other churches, come into being. Sometimes with the passing of the years they affiliate with "Antioch" or "Jerusalem." Sometimes they do not.

In short, whether encouraged or not, independent churches are actually arising on a large scale. As Christianity explodes across the world in ripening populations, particularly among cultured people inadequately reached by old-line Churches, we can expect this to happen more and more. As new forms of Christianity, which appeal to Hindus and Buddhists, arise, we can expect new departures which will dismay "Jerusalem" quite as much as the admission of uncircumcised pig-eaters did in Paul's day.

The indigenous Church has long been a goal of missions—but it was always a planned indigenous Church. The aim was to take the churches established under some Western pattern, and lead them to adopt such indigenous ways as commended themselves to the Western trained leadership. This had the advantage of being controlled and the disadvantage of proceeding very slowly. The other means of achieving "indigeneity" is to regard with tolerant eye the independent churches which arise—harking back to our Lord's saying, "For he who is not against us is for us" and His parable of the wheat and the tares growing together in one field.

When we see the very great variety of opinion within member Churches of various Fellowships and Councils of Churches—some practising baptism by sprinkling infants, others only by immersion upon profession of faith, and some not at all; some believing the Bible is literally inspired, others that we have only the approximate words of Jesus our Lord; some holding that every layman is able to celebrate the Lord's Supper, others that only correctly ordained priests in the apostolic succession can do so, we cannot help but believe that great charity should be observed toward the new Churches which will inevitably arise as Christ is accepted by groups and populations according to their own understanding.

As this process goes forward each existing Church will also expand by leading men into its own approved pattern. It is inconceivable that the present Churches will sit back and permit all growth to be into new groups outside any formal church connection. "Barnabas" will constantly be sent to "those who have received the grace of God at Antioch." "Paul," coming through some upper country, will constantly be finding a dozen disciples at "Ephesus" or the churches at "Puteoli" and "Rome." Furthermore, existing churches today will do exactly what the Antioch church did. When they find an indigenous pattern which works, they will put it into practice in a responsive population. Old and new patterns will both be followed.

There is a tendency for uniting Churches to speak of themselves as *the* Church, and of others as "sects." There will doubtless come a time when half the Protestants in America belong to one Church. How will that Church regard the Churches which maintain a separate life? As equally valid Churches, entitled by Christian love and religious freedom to all the courtesies and rights which itself enjoys; or as divisive sects? When United Churches arise in other lands, embracing the majority of the Christians, will they regard the rest as equally valid Churches or as inferior Christians? Will they regard the "True Jesus" churches, the "*Iglesia Ni Christo*," and the "No Church congregations"—as sects or as Churches? We are concerned that the pressure toward church union shall not predispose uniting Churches to denounce new independent Churches as enemies of the faith simply because they arise separately, and do not conform to the existing pattern.

Members of United churches should maintain that all Churches—whether in any given union or not—which believe on Jesus Christ as Lord and Saviour, and accept the Bible as the rule of faith and practice, are valid Christian Churches. Otherwise church union itself is divisive. It unites in one direction to divide in another. Leslie Newbiggin in *The Household of God* maintains that any Church treads on dangerous ground when it presumes to judge invalid any other Church which accepts Christ and the Scriptures and manifests the fruits of the Spirit in its life. If the pronouncement of this eminent bishop of the Church of South India guides United Churches, the attitude toward new independent Churches will be such that great growth will be encouraged and permitted. In the coming period of increasing responsiveness to the Gospel in country after country, all who are not against us are for us. We must make provision not only for entry into the established moulds, but into many moulds yet to be established. We must encourage those who hear the Gospel to start churches where they are, with the understanding of the Scriptures and the infilling of the Holy Spirit vouchsafed to them; confident that truth will triumph and not afraid of "expansion ahead of the Church."

XXI

FATIGUE

My friend met me at the railroad and we walked twenty miles to the headquarters of the constellation of 101 congregations. It was one of the most rapidly growing Churches in that part of the world. I wanted to find out what made it tick. We passed several mud and wattle chapels. "There are nine more back up that road and a dozen in this valley," he explained, "but don't take those figures as authoritative. The congregations have been growing so fast and boundaries between them have shifted so frequently that those are approximate numbers."

"What are your principal duties here?" I asked. "The usual thing," he answered. "I collect the offerings, add the mission grant, pay the men, visit the congregations with the greatest problems, discuss relocations with the village pastors who must be moved, and leaders in their congregations, examine candidates for baptism, see about the building and repair of new chapels, administer the sacraments, write our headquarters, chair the various councils and try to implement their minutes and actions."

"Why don't you get other qualified churchmen to carry part of the load?" I queried. "If you divided this field among four supervising ministers, each of you would still have a full load."

"No ordained minister to be had, foreign or national," he answered. "Our Church sends missionaries to the central training institutions and cannot afford to pay the salaries of highly trained nationals, besides which, the kind of men from East or West who will live and work in this deep rural section are rare birds. The Church considers this a one-man job. Some of the new village pastors are excellent leaders. But, of course, they have been non-Christians most of their lives and think and act differently from Christians with twelve or sixteen years schooling behind them."

"With a leadership like that, you have lots of problems?" I ventured. "Problems," he smiled. "I often think I shall go crazy, but the good Lord gives me grace to carry on. To be fair, the churches are prospering. Services are held regularly, little schools are taught in the chapel, and a new Bible-reading generation is being reared."

"What are you doing to expand the Church?" I asked innocently. "Are you getting enough converts?"

"Good heavens, man," he exploded, "this Church is in the midst of runaway expansion. I am honestly praying God that we have no more converts for a long time. We simply cannot handle them. It's no good baptizing them, if you cannot shepherd them. I've made it a rule never to baptize a new group unless I can give them a pastor—and I have absolutely run out of laymen who would do as village pastors. We have simply got to stop for a long, long period of consolidation."

This is a case of fatigue in the carrying out of the Great Commission. Wherever striking increase occurs, those responsible soon become overwhelmed with growth. It is a common phenomenon.

This fatigue is not primarily physical. There is, to be sure, hard work connected with the expansion of the churches. Tremendous amounts of footwork are called for, ceaseless touring, struggling up and down hills, swimming rivers, pounding the sidewalks, keeping all manner of hours, days and night. Sheer bodily weariness is involved, but the fatigue is not primarily physical.

As people of the world become Christian they bring in with them worldly habits, customs, reactions, emotions, and organizations. The Christian life is new to them. It cannot be otherwise. Regular congregational worship, for example, involves a cluster of new decisions and habits. Christian sex standards require major readjustments. The congregations demand constant guidance. The care of the churches, which Paul found so pressing, is no less pressing today. Ceaseless problems dance on the bed all through the night.

They are magnified by the tension between perfecting and discipling. Most churchmen used of God to extend the Church have been reared, as Paul was, "after the strictest fashion of the Pharisees." They are a very select group. Their standards of what Christians ought to be are high. It hurts them deeply to find even a few Christians quarrelling, drinking, dancing, gambling, and driving out one woman to take in another. It distresses them that any Christian should become nominal, slack in attendance, or slip now and again into old magical practices.

The younger Churches practise church discipline. Men and women are tried for the more serious sins. If found guilty, they are fined, debarred from communion, or excommunicated. The churchman in charge carries the responsibility for church discipline, which may include purging the church in a series of trials, each one fraught with emotional overtones. If the local church backs the offender, the churchman may have to put the entire congregation out of the fellowship. This is a grave burden.

These are some of the elements of fatigue. As converts increase and the congregations multiply, so do these problems, tensions, and responsibilities. Churchmen in a growing church area commonly express sorrow that their predecessors allowed the churches to grow so greatly, with such little oversight, such low standards, and such an accumulation of insoluble problems. "Whatever you do," they are likely to exclaim, "don't let your churches multiply too greatly." This is not wisdom speaking. This is fatigue.

Fatigue is a danger signal. The breaking-point has been reached. To the churchman concerned, it means "stop ingathering unless reinforcements are brought up." The churchman will do his best, create as much leadership as possible, squeeze the last possible penny out of the funds, count his own health of no value, but there is a point beyond which he cannot go.

The breaking point varies for different men and situations. The drive and the health of the man, his conviction, the amount of perfection he expects, the receptivity of the people, whether they respond individually, or by group, the quality of the new leadership available, and the degree to which it is entirely self-supporting or requires subsidy from the Mother Church—all these and other factors help determine the point at which fatigue sets in. In individual ingathering this may be when the communicant membership rises to 100–500. Where the method of entry is group conversion, the average breaking-point is at about 1,000 to 2,000 communicants.

Fatigue is caused by lack of resources (men and money) *at the point where the church is growing*. It is not caused, however, by lack of resources in the World Church. The Church—including both older and younger Churches—has abundant resources. It annually spends hundreds of millions of dollars. It has tens of thousands of competent, trained, and experienced churchmen. It has churchmen of every complexion, speaking every tongue, living on every conceivable standard of living, and citizens of every nation on earth. To get these abundant resources to the place of church-growth is a matter of a business efficiency.

Why should a chapter on fatigue be included in a section on the organizational factors controlling church-growth? It properly belongs here for several reasons. Fatigue is often the result of having to try to meet overwhelming opportunity with limited resources. It is the result of a lack of over-all direction.

For example, Nakoda faces a responsive people. In seven years God has added 10,000 to the Church there. Other ingathering has taken place in other stations of this Church-Mission, but none quite as large as that in Nakoda. Opportunity for growth continues. The limited number of churchmen facing many problems in these new congregations begin to say, "We simply must not take in many more. Character is more important than numbers. We must stop to consolidate. Quality, not quantity, must be the watchword." Churchmen concentrate on schools, the seminary, lifting the standard of health, and the like. The curve of growth levels off. Indeed in some places the number of Christians declines.

We might grant that three churchmen at Nakoda (for educational, medical, and church work) are justified: 10,000 new communicants probably are about as much as they can handle, maybe more than they should attempt. But is this Church-Mission justified in permitting a responsive people to go unreaped?

We might on investigation grant that, since the entire field in all stations is responsive, and all church headquarters are somewhat burdened with the care of the new churches, the Church-Mission is also justified in its use of the existing staff; but would deem them unworthy stewards in the degree to which they failed to point out the great opening to their own and all other boards.

The National Christian Council shares responsibility. If a responsive population anywhere in its territories is going unreaped, it has the privilege to sound the tocsin, call for reinforcements, and take up the question of reassignment of territories. Bringing responsive sections of the population into the fold is part of national organization of resources.

Consider the Mission Board involved. It may be that its activities have been pursued in due proportion so far as it can see God's will. But will He judge it blameless if it did not search far and wide, throughout Christendom, among all the congregations of earth, for the men and money which would have brought this generation at Nakoda into the Kingdom?

Finally, is there any body of men at the world level to whom the international missionary organizations have assigned the task of constant measurement of both responsiveness and available resources, so that maximum power is delivered where greatest church-growth can be obtained?

We could do with a "Harvestometer," an electronic brain, perhaps (for there is no time to lose, and speed in calculation is highly desirable) into which information concerning responsiveness and available resources is fed and out of which reliable direction for numbers of workers needed, their training, and their goals pours forth?

The World Mission at present has no clearing house for such information, no research centre which ceaselessly assembles such information and preserves reliable estimates of responsiveness and resources. The World Mission could have such a centre. Lack of it is a major error of organization. The World Mission limps along, groping its way in the dark. In the very places where the Church could double and treble in a decade, there resources are the least. Fatigue takes command. Workers cease to reap ripe fields. Where, on the other hand, the Church appears to have stopped growing, there resources are the greatest, vitality is high, and all sorts of new enterprises are put into operation. Yes, organization is influenced by fatigue.

XXII

"THE SAME FOR ALL"

On a rising national economy, with booming factories and multiplying people, church income rises. Ecclesiastical enterprises have more income. One mission board, sharing in its Church's general prosperity, finds that it has $50,000 more, an increase of 5 per cent over the last year. "How shall we use this sum?" asks the chairman of the Division of World Mission. The secretaries responsible for Africa, Latin America, China and Japan, South-East Asia, and Oceania know of many pieces of mission work which desperately need more funds. Each presents his case forcefully. After much discussion, the Division decides that each secretary for his field shall receive approximately 5 per cent more than he had last year. This is "the same for all" policy. The Division is like a mother with many children—each clamouring for food. The bigger the mission the more effective its pressures on the parent—and the greater its share. To satisfy all, the Division falls back on "the same for all."

On a falling national economy when mission budgets must be cut, the same procedure is followed in reverse. If three fields are concerned, with budgets from abroad of $100,000, $200,000 and $20,000, and the board's income has fallen by 10 per cent, these fields will be cut $10,000, $20,000 and $2,000 respectively. This is "the same for all."

It applies all the way down the line, starting with the top. The Church has several departments—the ministry, Christian education, home missions, world mission, social action, and administration. Each receives a more or less regular percentage of the total church income. The proportion cannot easily be changed. Year after year and decade after decade it remains about the same. The division of world mission takes its share and divides it proportionately among its missions and younger Churches. Each of these takes what it gets and wrestles with distribution. Since any change means taking funds away from fund-hungry projects, each of which is doing "a splendid piece of work," in the end each gets its due proportion. This is "the same for all" process which has ruled missions round the world.

It applies not merely to the money concerned, but also to the missionaries sent, building funds raised, number of nationals sent for study in the West, amount of space given in the church press to each enterprise, and many other matters. We use the financial aspect merely because it provides a good illustration.

Now obviously, "the same for all" policy is in part defensible. Any responsible organization guarantees its enterprises reasonable continuity. Also obviously, the process is not mechanically sealed. Changes do occur. Vivid personalities pull larger funds. Some great new need captures the popular imagination—usually some kind of disaster which gets a great play in the secular press—and new funds are raised specifically for that enterprise. Bishops, executive secretaries, and administrators favour the enterprises they judge worthy and frown on those they judge unworthy—or like or dislike.

Nevertheless, by and large, "the same for all" policy rules. Funds are frozen at definite percentages. In 1925 one great mission board, out of its total budget for foreign missions, spent 3.1 per cent in its most fruitful field. In 1930 the percentage was 3.0; in 1935 2.8; in 1940 2.9; in 1945 2.7; in 1950 2.9 and in 1955 2.7! During these years, depression and war had wracked the world, the Asian revolution had exploded, and Africa had started her march toward full self-government. Younger Churches had come into being as a brand new factor. Some fields of this board had proved lastingly sterile; others had demonstrated enormous potential growth. Yet, through it all, the most fertile field continued to receive a percentage fixed in those first and very different decades of the century.

The enterprises which survive are those which have representation on the budget committee. This is usually composed of those responsible for various pieces of work. These representatives bring to the budget session all their plans for continuation or expansion. There, in a meeting opened with prayer, men and women dedicated to the Church, each one earnestly desiring the coming of the Kingdom, plan the budget, estimate the available resources, and divide them among the constituent enterprises. Each budget is scrutinized by the entire group. Each member knows that what his enterprises receive depends largely on other enterprises getting about what they did last year. So each sees to it that the apple cart is not upset.

On a rising budget, when there is new money, new departures are possible. The committee hears various pleas from its members that their enterprises be favoured in the distribution of new money. None asks for favour, of course; they simply present some tremendously urgent proposal! Persuasive or popular members are likely to get more than their share, particularly if they do not ask too much in any given year. Courteous persistence also frequently wins the day. The parable of the importunate widow has been well studied by successful committee members. But, even on a rising budget, most of the new money will be budgeted equally for increases in all workers' salaries, repairs to property and increase in staff in all departments.

On a falling budget, tension rises. "Whose budget will be cut? Not mine." The chairman or treasurer tries to place the cuts where they will hurt the least. Some stronger members, and those who feel that their work is more important, try to get off with less of the cut. But the committee is made up of people who do not take kindly to the idea that any one work is "more important." Sometimes the reduction is made from a section of the enterprise which appears really weak or ineffective, but for the most part a little is taken off each budget. The younger Church or mission tightens its belt and goes on.

The process of distribution of resources is heavily loaded in the direction of the *status quo*. The Church or Mission is seldom in danger of too rapid shift. The danger is almost always that of frozen percentages and only creeping change.

How does all this effect church-growth?

As we have repeatedly pointed out, most church or mission enterprises are launched for the growth or welfare of the Church. They never get started unless some group of dedicated men and women judge them necessary for the general good of the Church. However (*a*) the "general good of the Church," like charity, covers a multitude of matters; (*b*) the group may be right, moderately right, or mistaken in the judgement; and (*c*) times change. Project P, under its first leader, was a very different thing from what it is now under its tenth. The kind of work needed when no one was becoming Christian is very different from that needed when hundreds are. Change is needed, but "the same for all" policy makes change an uphill business.

This system might work if the growth of the churches took place at a steady trickle wherever there was a piece of mission work. Indeed, that is what this system is planned for. And sometimes this occurs. Some Churches do grow by just a quiet general increase all along the line. Blessed are they! It is a comforting way in which to grow. But by and large Churches do not grow this way. They grow like water rising in a valley and spreading across the landscape. Where the banks are steep, the river rises a good deal without much spread, but when it reaches level fields, it races across them spreading more in ten minutes than it had in many hours before. "The same for all" attitude meets such racing opportunity with leaden feet. It cannot conceive that opportunity for church-growth is any more important than all its other works. Even if it could, it would be helpless to divert resources. "We would like to help you," this system would say, "but our many commitments simply will not permit it." It would speak truly.

The system offers one solution for the most urgent needs of the missionary enterprise—raising more money. "If a need is really urgent," it says, "go to the churches. Get through the boards and finance committees and appeal to the churches." In reality this is no solution because, first, it takes too much time; second, those working at places of church-growth are seldom men high in the council of the ecclesiastical organization concerned; third, any new approach to the churches must pass well armed guards. In short, "equalitarianism" neither diverts resources to meet rising needs nor permits new resources to be tapped. Unless measures are taken, "equalitarianism" alone will neutralize many factors favourable to church-growth. This is actually happening all around the world today.

Note that the power of "the same for all" system lies in unfocused missions. Where a dozen philosophies of missions, and a great spread of activities, all justify themselves by different criteria, there "equalitarianism" achieves a death-grip. But "the same for all" system is weak where men can say with Bishop Stephen Neill: "The missionary should regard the winning of men for Christ as ten times more important than anything else he does. The total evangelization of great regions is the main task. You must move in that dimension of thought or else you can make no sense of missions," or where men can pray the following line, taken out of a worship service in a small Indiana town: "Grant that through the work of our missionaries, men everywhere may be led to confess Christ."

What measures should be taken where "the same for all" system is found? The first measure is to make its nature and consequences crystal clear. As soon as evangelical clergymen recognize it they will loosen its control. They will keep what is good in it and circumvent what is evil. They will exercise control over their budgets. They will be on the alert for opportunities of church-growth and make provision for them. They earnestly desire church increase: they will administer the sacred funds that this may come about. They will do this at the level of the division of world missions, the mission, the stations, the younger Church, and its parishes.

The second measure is for mission boards so to manage the enormous funds passing annually through their hands, that they can meet sudden opportunities for church-growth as they arise. A reserve for church-growth of, perhaps, 10 per cent of the total income will be set up. No responsible board will be unable to advance into one of its ripened fields. Every opportunity, on the contrary, will find adequate resources prepared ahead of time for it. Extreme care will be used that such reserves are spent only for church-growth. Churchmen on these special resources will operate under a mandate to produce church-growth.

Third, the upper levels of organization, provincial and national Christian Councils, Federations of Churches, Fellowships of Evangelicals, and the like, will keep a priority list. On bright red paper they will indicate those areas of the field in which homogeneous units have been growing by any method whatsoever, in any population, at the rate of 100 per cent a decade or more. Possibly they might set different norms for different regions: 200 per cent increase for Africa; 100 per cent for the Philippines, and 60 per cent for the Buddhist world. They would make it their highest responsibility to keep any younger Church on the Red List fully supported. At

XXIII

ADMINISTRATION AND CHURCH-GROWTH

Can a board secretary on one side of the ocean, or a general secretary of the Church on the other, administer resources so as to achieve church-growth? Can a mission or younger church, a station or a missionary, so manage its affairs that churches multiply?

Some administrators answer, "No, the task of the administrator is to see that funds keep on coming in and are spent in a wide variety of enterprises which have commended themselves to the six groups concerned—congregations, older Church, board, mission, younger Church, and younger Churches' congregations. A good administrator keeps the machine running smoothly, without using it to the undue advantage of any part of the whole undertaking."

"Besides which," they may even continue, "church-growth is an elusive thing. It cannot be produced here or there at will. Good administrators place well trained churchmen in their fields. They build up an organization—mission or Church or both—so that educated responsible Christians are reared whose children continue in the Faith. In this process churches will grow naturally, as they can. If they do not, the administration is not to blame. There are many unripe fields and God gives the increase as He wills. Our task is simply to see that the Gospel is proclaimed by every means available and the resulting churches nurtured."

This answer is seldom put into words, but it accounts for much present administration. Is it a correct answer?

We believe it is far too wide a generalization. It dogmatizes for all younger Churches and mission fields in all stages of development. It may be good in a few fields; but it is debatable in others, and in some it is unsatisfactory.

It arbitrarily reduces church-growth to a by-product which may or may not occur in a successful mission, when in reality church-growth is the central continuing purpose of the world mission.

Can administrators then use the resources at their command to achieve church-growth?

Let us avoid generalizations and deal with three specific instances. Let churchmen examine them in the light of their own situation.

First, let us take the Southern Baptist growth in Formosa, already described.

The Southern Baptists entered the island in 1949 with one missionary and perhaps 200 Christians. They have administered this field for church-growth. They would heartily dissent from the answer given to the question which opened our chapter. They have established a well-staffed seminary to produce Mandarin-speaking Chinese pastors in abundance. They carry on an active programme of evangelism, where it will win converts. These come for the most part as individuals in cities and small towns. The Southern Baptists send to Formosa missionaries whose purpose is bringing men and women into redeeming fellowship with Christ. They spend little time and money in auxiliary services. They put in no more resources than many a Church does in many a land, but what they put in is focused on church-growth. In 1956 they had over 4,000 baptized believers and about 3,000 catechumens under instruction. Their leading churchmen expect this kind of growth to continue.

What principles of administration did the Southern Baptists follow:

(1) They sent resources to where churches were growing. In 1949 they had only one missionary and one small congregation in Formosa. As fertility was proved, they pressed in with more.

(2) They sent churchmen who believed in great commission missions like those of the United Presbyterians in the Punjab in 1882 and the Methodists in Ashanti in 1922.

(3) They trained their men for this kind of mission and set them to work to multiply churches.

(4) They were more afraid of not harvesting a ripened field than of reaping by a "second-best" method. They did not let the doctrine of "full self-support from the beginning" deflect them from planting churches. They have subsidized as much as was necessary to get churches going. They have put considerable funds into church buildings. When asked, "Is this good mission policy?" they reply, "We wanted a larger degree of self-support; but if the present degree of giving continues while these congregations double and treble in membership, full self-support will be achieved in a few years.

Perhaps our way of starting is not the best way, but it is better than not starting at all."

(5) Seeing the Mandarin-speaking field unoccupied and unworked by the Presbyterians, whose churches were all Amoy speaking, the Baptists did not permit comity to deny them entry to a ripe but unworked field.

Each of these five points required administrative decisions at the level of the American seminary, the mission board, the mission in Formosa, and the younger Church. Had all the decisions—or indeed any one of them—been made in the wrong direction, the Baptists would not be rejoicing in great church growth in Formosa. *The chain of correct administrative decisions in a ripe population is obtaining good sound church growth which should measure over* 1,000 *per cent in a decade.* Administration did in this case secure church growth.

Second, let us take an illustration from a more complicated situation. Younger Church J of 40,000 communicants and 400 churches has 40 ministers who are seminary graduates and 360 village pastors of about fifth grade education plus two years in a Bible School. It raises three-fourths of the pay of the village pastors and one-half of the pay of the seminary graduates, some of whom occupy posts previously held by missionaries. It is assisted by a staff of 40 missionaries and a work budget of $80,000 from abroad. It has 3 hospitals, 4 high schools, 200 primary schools, 1 arts college and 1 Bible School. It has a share in a Union Theological Seminary.

The Church as a whole has grown at 10 per cent for the last decade. The Church consists of 5 homogeneous units. J1 of 15,000 communicants is losing ground, J2 and J3 of 9,000 and 8,000 are standing still. J4 is making 60 per cent growth and J5 had quadrupled in the decade, doubling in the last three years. All 5 Churches do a great deal of evangelism.

Of its 80 leading churchmen (40 nationals and 40 missionaries) 20 are pastors of non-growing churches, 45 are in institutional posts, 6 are in the general administration of the Church, 5 are superintendents of the five districts, and 4 are pastors of growing churches in J4. Of mission funds only 4 per cent goes to help the congregations that are growing. The pastors and laymen of growing congregations in J4 and J5 say, "If we had a lot more leaders and a lot more help in evangelism there could be tremendous growth here."

In this specific situation, can administration increase church-growth? Or must it be content to nurture the Church-Mission machine, confident that some growth, as God wills, will naturally occur here and there? It is always in such specific and differing situations that the question must be asked.

Suppose the following steps were taken. They may not be the best, but are at least possible. What would happen?

(1) J5 has only one seminary graduate in it—the district superintendent. Three vigorous seminary graduates, however, could be used to advantage as his assistants. It has 20 Bible-School graduate village pastors: to grow at the present 400 per cent it must have 30 more at once.

(2) J4 has 5 seminary graduates but could use 3 more immediately. It has 60 Bible-School graduates but could use 20 more at once and still 40 more if a new ripe area were entered.

(3) Six volunteers are called for from among the 45 institutional churchmen to accept assignment in J4 and J5 as supervisors of rapid expansion in areas where one supervisor and 5 village pastors will be located in anticipation of growth.

(4) All churchmen in J4 and J5 meet frequently to discuss what is making the churches increase and to pray for ingathering.

(5) Out of the very considerable building funds from abroad, $5,000 a year is set aside to buy galvanized iron sheets to roof any chapel for which the new congregation erects the walls.

(6) Forty scholarships a year are made available at the Bible School and from the 8,000 communicants in J4 and J5, 40 men are selected to go there for a two year course: 10 additional men are sent to Seminary.

(7) Great stress is laid on stewardship and self-support.

(8) One-tenth of the laymen of each church in J4 and J5 are given a month's training in proclamation of the Gospel to unbelievers during the slack agricultural month of the year.

(9) In J1 2 and 3 announcement is made that, should any of these Churches show real growth, similar action would be taken for them.

(10) All this presents the assisting board and Church J with need for $15,000 a year further funds. $3,000 is guaranteed by the Church. The Board by paring budgets and transfers provides $7,000. The remaining $5,000 cannot be met by the supporting board. It therefore searches for another mission, of a Church with a similar polity, to help produce maximum harvesting in the area of J5. Till such is found, the board makes a special effort and provides the remaining $5,000.

It is clear that if the desire is there, steps can be taken which will lead J4 and J5 into maximum growth. It is equally clear that, if the desire is not there, these steps will be judged impossible or undesirable, a limited amount of growth will occur but the situation will continue semi-static using 40 missionaries and $80,000 a year from the sending Church for decade after decade.

For a third illustration we take a small vigorous people-movement where there is, as yet, not much of a younger Church. In a tribe of 20,000, over a period of three years, 1,200 have become Christians in a series of group conversions. The senior churchman responsible (national or foreigner) has appointed ten village pastors and started a boarding-school at the station, in which forty boys are studying. What with putting up buildings, visiting new churches, running the school, instructing village pastors and laymen, examining and baptizing inquirers, settling quarrels, and disciplining backsliders, the senior churchman is reaching the end of his strength. So far there is no competing Church in the area.

Can administration encourage growth here? It would be possible for it to take one of the following paths:

(*a*) To send the senior churchman a message like this: "We have so many commitments, that it is quite impossible to give you any further budget. We rejoice in your successes, but can hold out no hope of reinforcements." The outcome would be that a few hundred more would become disciples and then the movement would stop.

(*b*) To send a doctor, educationist, and agriculturist, intending that the all round team would increase church growth, or intending that it would merely care for those already discipled. There are instances, where, when sending new forces, administration has said, "These are to help you do a good job in the area you have occupied. Do not use them for extension. We are not going to start more than we can care for and any idea of five or six new outposts is quite impossible." While saying this, administration has not earnestly sought for aid from others either. It has simply dismissed the winnable as too big a job.

The outcome in either case would ordinarily be that the first worker would get busy building houses for the other three, do less instruction and touring than before and get tied up more and more in station affairs. The newcomers when settled would devote themselves to their specialists. As a result, after a few hundreds more had been baptized, growth would stop. "Great mission work" would, however, continue and visitors would thrill at the unselfish labours of churchmen in the far reaches of the world. Some 18,000 who could have been reached with the right help would remain undiscipled.

But suppose that, instead, administration took path (*c*) and decided:

(1) To send three foreign and three national workers as assistants to the senior churchman with instructions to stake out five further ripening areas in the tribe, each of about 4,000 population and to duplicate in them what had been done in the first. This action would intend to claim for Christ the total responsive population of 20,000.

(2) To put the senior churchmen, under whom the movement had begun to grow, in temporary charge of the whole development. The purpose of this would be to guarantee that incoming reinforcements did not destroy a successful pattern.

(3) To give him helpers in a Bible School to train several score village teacher-preachers.

(4) To transfer out of the area any national or foreign churchman under whom the Church in this rich situation did not grow.

(5) To chalk out a Ten-Year Plan in which supporting services (such as schools, hospitals, literacy campaigns, and agricultural programmes, according to the resources available) might be introduced.

It is not our purpose in the above to describe "the one correct procedure" for small vigorous people-movements. Correct procedures can only be determined on the ground, facing the actual situations and would, certainly, be more complex than these four simple actions. It is our purpose to indicate that in ripe fields, administration (which might be boards, or Churches, or stations or dioceses) has a wide variety of ways open to it. Some lead towards and others away from church-growth.

What then, in the field for which he is responsible, must the administrator do to achieve church-growth? The following suggestions are tendered. They apply on all levels—parish, station, diocese, and country.

(1) The administrator himself should sincerely desire church-growth. He should have a passion that men become disciples of Christ.

(2) He should discern and define ripe fields, recognizing that ripe parts of specific fields may be separate entities. He should keep before him charts showing growth. If he has a feeling that these are not sufficiently reliable, he should get substantiating reports. Great issues hang on accurate and up-to-date measurements.

(3) Administration should see that a balance is maintained between efforts in ripe and unripe fields—such a balance as the Saviour Himself will approve. Any weight in favour of the *status quo* should be avoided.

(4) Administration should recognize and reward church-growth.

(5) Administration should see that all available resources reach the ripest parts of the field in adequate amounts.

(6) Administration should insist that training in seminaries and missionary training institutes qualify churchmen to understand and achieve church-growth.

(7) Administration should encourage suitable forms of outreach so that new worshipping groups are constantly formed.

(8) Administration should manipulate the resources of advice, men, and money, so that the central continuing purposes of missions—the carrying out of the great commission—is obtained.

(9) Administration should most particularly guide those working in auxiliary services so that the 3,000 of Pentecost continue "in the apostles' teaching, and fellowship, breaking of bread and prayers," *while they become* 50,000.

From the church-growth point of view, the central problems of administration at all four levels is: how can Christian administrators avoid diversion of efforts to secondary ends? How can they keep attention centred on discipling the nations?

There is no simple answer to this key question. This entire book, written out of thirty years' experience of administration, on the level of the station, the younger Church, and the Mission, comes back again and again to the extremely complex nature of the task. We have pointed out how under some circumstances administration can break through to church-growth. Ours is not a complete answer. Nevertheless, we are confident that, in ripe fields, administration can lead out into great church-growth if it is ready to seek for ways and means. It can lead away from great church-growth even without trying to do so. Indeed, if it does nothing but carry on the traditional tasks, it will as effectively prevent church-growth as if it had consciously ruled against it.

Can the quarter-back or captain advance the ball down the field? We answer, "That is his principal function. He administers the team so that the ball advances, yards are gained, and points scored. Facing a given formation, he may send the play left, right, forward, or even backward, but the intent will be to gain yards. He knows that his success is not going to be measured by the skill with which he keeps the team moving, the precision of his plays, or the goodwill of his players. It is going to be measured by touchdowns and field goals."

Can administration bring about church-growth? We answer, "This is precisely its principal function. In the changing shifting situation from month to month and year to year, with the initiative sometimes in our hands and sometimes in those of the 'other team,' administration makes hundreds of decisions, right, left, forward, and even backward, but all calculated to multiply churches. Administration on every level of younger and older Churches will be measured by the degree of success achieved."

CONCLUSION

How Churches Grow—The New Frontiers of Mission has been written in the midst of a tremendous crisis in missions.

Since 1800 missions have been intimately involved with colonialism. Missions have gone from the rulers to the ruled, from industrialized to agricultural nations, and from the culturally advanced to the culturally retarded. They could not have done otherwise. Today's advance of the non-Occident and the break up of colonialism leaves missions and younger Churches searching in scores of ways for a whole new mode of mission which shall be from free and equal nations to free and equal nations. So unprecedented are the problems that searching for solutions often becomes groping. Old land-marks are no longer there. Many solutions offered are no solutions. After being used for a short while they are discarded and others tried.

Missions are being carried on in the midst of the third great revolution of mankind, the first being that from a hunting to an agricultural economy, and the second the industrialization of the West. The third, marked by automation, atomic power, electronics, and a fantastic development of rockets and space travel, is upon us and is pushing nations hither and thither at bewildering speed.

The Church today faces a war-like and suddenly unified world. Very dissimilar nations are forced to live cheek by jowl with each other. The likelihood of war looms large. Different standards of living over-night become horrible injustices. Racial pride and animosity—innocuous when oceans intervened—simmer and bubble when oceans disappear. Hence the Church is pre-occupied with problems of working toward peace, brotherhood, justice, and plenty. Many churchmen cry that progress toward these is the present mission of the Church.

The older Churches and the younger Churches find themselves tied up with each other. Many a younger Church is (and may remain) in somewhat the same position as that of the children of

Israel on the return of the spies—unwilling or unable to advance. The younger Churches are usually weak and inexperienced. Sometimes, like some older Churches, they are static and ingrown. Yet, in their lands, they are the only Churches there are. The older Churches cannot move unless the younger Churches say so.

Little wonder that under such circumstances missions have so largely become colossal enterprises of inter-church aid. Everything impels toward that outcome.

Finally, the world mission today seethes with major theological debate. What, after all, is its theological basis? It cannot be cultural improvement or raising the standards of living of backward peoples. Missions never were defensible as part of "the white man's burden," though they do draw support from the idea of helping backward segments of mankind. What is there in God Himself which impels to mission—and would continue to impel, were Christians the poorest and most backward of all peoples? Should any propose to give up missions entirely and leave further Christianization to the younger Churches, we must ask him whether his solution is theologically right. Is it pleasing to God? We seek today for theological foundations. What, for example, is the theological meaning of conversion? What is the theological significance of "the ends of the earth"? Is a foreign missionary society a theological necessity for all Churches, East and West, or is it a historical convenience? These and many other questions and issues in one form or another recur in the formal and informal studies now going on round the world.

No wonder that the characteristic of missions today is a puzzled defensiveness. A noted writer on missions expresses this mood when he affirms that "no one knows just what mission is today." Yet all agree that the vast enterprise must be carried forward and, indeed, increased.

Most books on mission today deal chiefly with the revolutionary changes and the need to adjust to younger Churches, to fit new independent nations, to correct theological attitudes toward the living faiths, to justify mission as inter-church aid or world friendship, to help the masses get more of this world's goods, or to rectify various displacements caused by new alignments.

We have no mind to gainsay the reality and importance of these revolutionary changes. A great deal has been written on them. Conferences talk ceaselessly about them. Often Christians become so absorbed in them that they tend to forget what mission is. Therefore in the midst of all this tumult—about which we have said but little—this book fastens attention on the continuing goal. Persuading men to become disciples of Christ, and responsible members of His Church, is beyond doubt a chief part of mission, and will continue so. The reality and importance of this truth cannot be gainsaid. Hence we plead the following major propositions:

(1) We face a ripening world in which population after population, in land after land, is reaching out for salvation in Christ. These populations for various reasons are now winnable. Significant numbers of men and women from them can become our fellow disciples. Significant numbers of churches of Christ can be planted.

(2) God has willed this ripening world. It is no accident. Hence He also wills that fields white to harvest be sought out and reaped to the last sheaf. This ripening world has theological significance. What we do with responsive persons is done in the sight of the Saviour and in the light of the Cross.

(3) Such harvesting has nothing to do with a secular hunger for numbers, power, this world's transient glory, or men's praise. On the contrary, it rises out of obedience to God and involves passionate participation in the purpose of our Saviour. Christian harvest occurs as He indwells us.

(4) Hence the indwelt should take church-growth with life-and-death seriousness. We must be about the Saviour's business with intensity, dedication, and sacrifice. Facing both responsive populations and vast mounting populations "out of Christ and His Church," winning men to Christian commitment, can never be one of many equally good ends. It is that for which our Lord went to the Cross. It has eternal urgency.

As every nation becomes a neighbour of every other, the parable of Lazarus and the account of the Last Judgement must not be limited to supplying physical food to the physically hungry. After all, our Lord said plainly, "Do not fear those who kill the body but cannot kill the soul; rather fear him who can destroy both body and soul in hell." According to the Bible, the supreme need of any men anywhere is for redeeming faith in Christ. How much keener is that need and how much greater our responsibility before God in cases where it is a conscious need, and men, lying at our very doors, beg to be discipled now.

(5) Discipling the nations in populations large and small is the surest way to social progress. We categorically reject any alleged antagonism between evangelism and social action. The reorganization of society on more Christian lines will be enormously furthered by massive accessions to the Christian Faith. No factor will play so great a part in social advance as the conscience of practising disciples of Christ.

(6) Since, in the processes of mission, as in other human endeavours, self-deceit is a constant possibility, we should shun rationalizations which substitute something else, "just as good" and much less demanding, for discipling the nations.

(7) Since times and situations change while the urgency of proclamation of Christ and persuasion to follow Him remain, we subject our aims, presuppositions, budget allocations, and church and mission policies to continuing scrutiny as to their relation to harvest. This is particularly necessary where these arise outside a given country, or where churchmen, by virtue of their employment or long practice, have a vested interest in church or mission work which is not accompanied by church-growth.

(8) Extensive study of church-growth is an urgent necessity. All churchmen, from those in lonely outposts to those in great Christian councils, should study the multiplication of churches with painstaking care. It is complex and seldom proceeds according to commonly accepted ideas in Western circles. We should labour to discern how God is now at work among the ripening harvests to bring men to Christian commitment and faithful church-membership. Abundant funds—probably 1 per cent of all expenditures—should be allocated to such study and the publication and dissemination of findings.

(9) Reliable accounting of church-memberships (gains by transfer, baptisms from the world and from the churches; and losses by death, discipline, removals, and reversions) should be instituted, and serious attention paid to it. As both younger and older Churches, conscious that membership is one chief criterion of success in

mission, assemble reliable figures, they will at least have the facts on which to work for maximum ingathering.

(10) In all moot questions—and their name is legion—decision should be sought not on the basis of Western or Eastern culture, the sanctions of time-honoured procedures, grounds of expediency or convenience, or to suit older or younger Churches or their leaders, but on the unshakable ground of God's revelation in Jesus Christ our Lord. Here it is that the relationship of the Word of God to the Living Religions of mankind, the authority and urgency of evangelism and conversion, and the priorities of various programmes can be determined. We have Jesus Christ our Lord. We have no one else. We have the Bible. We have nothing else. In the Light of revelation we can go fearlessly forward.